" A LOOK BEHIND
THE TIP
OF THE ICEBERG "

To Beverly Johnson
This is about the past that
I hope makes the future
brightly.

[signature]

"A LOOK BEHIND
THE TIP
OF THE ICEBERG"

By

Lionel Fultz

{A graphic description that unmasks "CORPORATE
AMERICA'S" conspiracy against African-American
employee's.}

ISBN 1-58820-018-3

1stBooks Rev. 6/19/00

ABOUT THE BOOK

"If this is ever published, it would be like throwing a hand grenade into the middle of corporate America." A quote from the 1st publisher that read "A Look Behind the Tip of the Iceberg." The author, IBM's first African-American Salesman and Branch Manager, holds nothing back in describing, through actual experiences, Corporate America's policies to tolerate but deny an equal opportunity to African American employee's. Like a dictionary, it should be on the desk of all corporate employees', both present and future.

To those, over the centuries, both known and unknown, who made the supreme sacrifice to bring equal treatment to all.

THE YEAR IS 1997

AFTER AGREEING TO PAY $176.1 MILLION TO SETTLE
A RACIAL DISCRIMINATION SUIT, THE CHAIRMAN
AND C.E.O. OF TEXACO MADE THE FOLLOWING
STATEMENT ON CNN'S "LATE EDITION":

"RACIAL DISCRIMINATION PROBLEMS AT HIS
COMPANY REPRESENT JUST THE TIP OF THE ICEBERG
IN CORPORATE AMERICA"

MY EXPERIENCE AS IBM'S 1ST AFRICAN AMERICAN
SALESMAN AND BRANCH MANAGER COVERS THE
PERIOD FROM 1950 TO MY RETIREMENT AND OFFERS
"THAT LOOK BEHIND THE TIP OF THE
ICEBERG".

x

CONTENTS

"A Look Behind THE TIP OF THE ICEBERG"

FORWARD

Since my retirement in January,1984, many of my friends, both within and outside of IBM, having some knowledge of my experiences while with IBM, frequently encouraged me to write about them. For years I had many misgivings about taking on such a task. For one, I'm not a writer and don't pretend to be one. Secondly, I didn't feel that writing about my career would be interesting to others. However, after continuous urging from many of my friends, (who,if this is published better buy) sat down and typed twenty-five pages. I quickly tired and threw the script into the bottom drawer of my desk, where it soon got buried under other "throwaways" that I never threw away. This was over three years ago. A few months ago I decided to get rid of a lot of junk that had piled up in my desk in order to make room for more recent junk. That's when I discovered my forgotten twenty-five pages. After reading it, for the first time, I found it interesting but wasn't certain others would think likewise. Before I had a chance to refile the script, my wife's niece stopped by for a visit. She is a person who stays so busy that I can't remember the last time I saw her actually sit down and relax for more than ten minutes. I expected her to read a couple of pages, tell me it's great to be polite and then take off. What happened was totally unexpected by me. She focused on those twenty-five pages so intensely, that no one, including her young son who was present, could interrupt. She wanted to read the rest, but there was no rest, and I mean that. She used words to inflate my ego and caused me to continue where I left off. Continuing wasn't that pleasant, especially when it brought back many unpleasant memories. But life itself, wasn't that pleasant for most blacks trying to pursue careers in business fifty years ago.

When I was very young and trying to understand why so many people treated me differently and showed dislike because I was different, a sage told me that most people don't hate, but unfortunately many let the few that hate control them. When individuals are not fearful of making their own judgements and learn about others who seem different, prejudices gradually disappear. This I learned during my career with IBM. Despite the state of havoc many of my superiors constantly attempted to place me in, my strongest defenders were frequently those I managed, or as I always described them, (despite my position), as "those I work with". I always emphasized that they work for IBM, but we work together. Managers and others who reported to me, given the option of joining those in higher management who attacked me, always supported me, despite the risk of jeopardizing their careers.

One of my administration managers, who was caught in the middle of one of many battles with my superiors, went all out defending me during a very critical investigation. Gary Helsel was a former marine, strong and with high morals. Quoting Gary, when we later met: "Lionel, I just want to let you know that I didn't defend you because you're my boss, I defended you because you were right. If you were wrong, I would have done the opposite.". My reply was simply: "Knowing you, Gary, that is what I was always sure of". Bob Brady, Gary Helsel, Nancy Rutkowski, Jean Bateman and hundreds of others , despite pressures, made their own judgements and always offered their support. T. G. Laster, if your spirits around, any words of appreciation would only be a repetition of what our friendship expressed while you were here. Earl Wilson, a friend who has contributed so much to benefit others, always a giver and not a taker. I've heard historians say that knowing history in its true form, helps you understand why events evolved as they did. I've tried to relate events as I remember them. In writing my original manuscript, past events became clearer and easier to describe when using the names of individuals involved in my career with IBM. Most are now either deceased or retired. Considering present circumstances and having no desire to have my words stir hatreds or exact satisfaction from anyone for past actions, I have edited out most names. My desire is to relate an individual experience of an Afro-American in Corporate America when discrimination abounded not only in South Africa, but in the

United States, the "Cradle of Democracy". As many corporations are beginning to learn, "in today's climate, "Tokenism" against discrimination may appease the conscience of many corporations but does not prevent the filing of "class action" discrimination suits by minorities." It would give me great satisfaction if my words, in some way, pursuades Corporate America that it is more profitable in many ways to use the skills of all, regardless of their race, gender or ethnic background.

INTRODUCTION

1950 - A perspective of the "black" employment environment For those from my generation, there's no need to detail what the job opportunities were for blacks in 1950. The environment that existed then certainly would bring back unpleasant memories to them. Todays environment, 1997, though far from perfect, has improved, especially for those blacks who are fortunate enough to obtain marketable skills. For those of you who are not completely aware of what the "playing field" was like for blacks in Corporate America during my career from 1950 to 1984, the following is a brief and condensed picture of that environment. Being aware of these conditions perhaps will make the unbelievable, believable. The year 1950 was long before the era of Martin Luther King, the "lunch counter sit-ins in the south" and the civil right's marches. I lived in the Manhattan community of Harlem, which was 99.9% black. As an example, over 90% of the stores were owned and operated by white merchants. Despite the fact that all their customers were black, they still hired mostly white clerks in their stores. The salesmen who sold these merchants were practically all white, except for the beer and liquor industry. In the latter, there were just a handful of black salesmen, and most of those were restricted to black owned businesses. If you think that Harlem was a well of discrimination as compared to other communities throughout the United States, consider the following. In 1947, when I became a salesman for the Pabst Brewing Company, I became the fourth "black" beer salesman (of all company's) in Harlem. I knew of only two others in the rest of the country. One represented Pabst and the other Anheuser-Busch.

Black physicians, dentists and funeral directors, for the most part, did well, since whites in those professions, during that period, didn't cater to the black community. The best jobs for blacks were in the postal service, a very few in local government, dining car waiters and pullman porters in the railroad industry and manual labor in heavy industry, such as automobiles and steel. The trade unions would not accept black apprentices, so even in black neighborhoods, if a licensed plumber, bricklayer, carpenter, or any other building tradesman was needed, they had to be white.

In some metropolitan areas of the south, black owned insurance company's flourished, since most company's wouldn't insure blacks and the few that did, received policies that cost more and provided less. Non-union black tradesmen, in some areas of the south, were able to make a living, since it wasn't acceptable for a white tradesman working for a black household.

You name the industry, IBM, Remington Rand, General Motors, Chrysler, Prudential, Metropolitan Life and all the other large corporations. I could name only two blacks in white collar positions. Thomas G. Laster, hired in 1946 as a Special Representative with IBM and C. Udell Turpin, hired in a similar position with Remington Rand.

Where were blacks employed? I knew many college graduates who were waiting on tables. Lawyers working as redcaps in train stations. (One eventually became one of the first black judges in New York City). Janitors, maintenance men, any legitimate way to support their families. And of course, those unable to find work, on welfare. And with the advent of ADC, (Aid for dependent children), a few fathers chose to abandon their families so their children could qualify for welfare. This had a devastating affect on those families.

In retrospect, in 1950, the leaders of Corporate America, the great pioneers of democracy throughout the world, fostered discrimination against blacks and of course women to a lesser degree. They, at least, got in the door. That is if they could type.

During my service in World War II, we heard of cases where the Commanding General (in this case George Patton}, relieved Division Commanders for failing to comply with directives. The 2nd Lieutenant commanding a platoon wasn't relieved nor any of the others under the Division Commander. Needless to say, his replacement followed orders and the objectives were met. In comparison, I found corporations similar in seeing that

xviii

directives were carried out, that is except when the directives pertained to "equal opportunities" for blacks. With the support of the Board of Directors, a Chief executive order sets policies and objectives for the company to meet. If the Chief executive officer, with the support of the board of directors, sets policies or objectives for the Division Vice Presidents to meet, unless their met or a good faith effort is shown, heads usually roll. In 1950 there were no policies or objectives to be met requiring the hiring of blacks, so nothing was done. With the Kennedy administration, in 1960, policies and objectives were set by many corporations when they signed pledges to the "Plans for Progress Program", designed to bring black employee's into their company's. In IBM the Chief Executive Officer, as with other company's, issued the directives. For the first time, nothing was done and no one was demoted or fired. In American industry, the same policies of discimination against blacks continued, thanks not to the subordinates who failed to carry out the orders, but to the "General's" who failed to discipline when their directives were not carried out.

As the Chairman of Texaco stated, "Racial discrimination problems at his company represent just the tip of the iceberg in Corporate America". The blame for the problems that exist today rest with those same boards and CEO'S that chose to ignore the failure of their management to carry out their orders. Hopefully, "A LOOK BEHIND THE TIP OF THE ICEBERG" will help all levels of management and future and present CEO's from repeating past mistakes. More important, for those who have a "sense of fair play" when all the facts are known, hopefully my experience will help you to understand why many Afro-Americans feel that despite some improvement, the playing field is still far from being level for them.

CHAPTER I

"LBJ's Helping Hand"

It's the early summer of 1963. John F. Kennedy is in his 3rd year as President of the United States and I'm in my 13th year with IBM, still pursuing my desire to be a sales manager. When Truman was challenged for the presidency by Thomas Dewey in the elections of 1947, many of my friends in New York City, who usually voted democratic, voted for Dewey. Not because they thought Dewey would be the better man for them, for they expected no benefits from either candidate. They voted for Dewey because Truman was a "white southerner" and was therefore considered the worst of the two. The same applied to Lyndon Johnson when he ran for Vice President but didn't affect my friends choice as much since Kennedy would be President and the Vice President's position was considered powerless.

As it turned out Truman made the first step towards integrating our society by integrating the armed services. Something Roosevelt or any high ranking politician or office holder, to my knowledge, ever suggested. I was wrong in my assessment of Truman and horribly wrong with that of Lyndon Johnson, as my future experiences proved. 1963 Here I am, sitting in my room at the Summit Hotel in Manhattan, waiting for a phone call from the assistant to the divisions personnel director, who is to escort me to a meeting of top IBM executives at the data processing divisions headquarters in White Plains, New York. The purpose of the meeting is to determine future strategy for a project that was ordered by IBM's Chairman of the Board and Chief Executive officer, Thomas J. Watson, Jr. I was expected to present a program that would accomplish the corporations objectives regarding the project. There were no bars or stars for me to polish, because after thirteen years with IBM, I still had not reached the position of manager. If an enlisted man meeting with a room full of generals, to advise

1

them how a project should be carried out sounds weird, it also tells you the drastic steps a corporation will take when their past policies roused the ire of the Vice President and future President of the United States, Lyndon B. Johnson. I was to soon learn that my escort, Walter Noe, was retired from the military and was considered a "trouble shooter" for some of the top executives in IBM. He was easy to recognize. My best guess is that he was pushing fifty, 5 ft. 9, and had to weigh close to 300 lbs. Despite his physical appearance, he was quick in moving, highly intelligent and very fast in getting things done. The story given to me was that Walter was recruited by a corporate vice president who was trying to clean up serious problems that were occuring in the division that was his responsibility. At the time, he was an administration manager at an IBM office in California and the Vice President was impressed by his quick response in tackling problems. His new position was like jumping a 2nd lieutenant to Major General, reporting only to the commanding general and having all headquarters staff taking orders from him. Walter once told me that he once drew a line on the floor in front of his desk, and ordered that no one was to cross that line. (This was confirmed to me by an executive who reported to him at the time}.

When the divisions problems were resolved and Walter's boss returned to the Corporate staff, Walter remained in the division as an assistant to the director of personnel. I later learned that Walter was still taking orders from top corporate executives. He didn't have the power he once had, but my impression was that he was "untouchable" because of his contacts.

It was the early summer of 1963 and a year since my promotion to IBM's Washington Federal office. I was not a manager but considered to be in management training.

I was to attend a meeting at IBM's Data Processing divisions headquarters in White Plains, New York. I had only arrived in New York the prior evening, and after meeting with the president of IBM's Office Products division, things were moving fast. I had no idea who I was meeting with or the purpose of the meeting. Walter Noe was assigned to bring me there. Since the

2

meeting wasn't until late that afternoon, Walter invited me to have lunch with him at a restaurant in mid-Manhattan. Before the hostess could leave, after seating us, Walter asked her to bring us a drink.According to the rules I was taught regarding drinking on the job, I ordered coffee while Walter ordered a double martini.

Just 24 hours ago, while making a call at the Goddard Space Flight center in Maryland, I received a message to call my office asap. I was told to drop whatever I was doing, drive immediately to National Airport in Washington, and take the first shuttle to New York City. Gordon Moodie, President of IBM's office products division, wanted me to report to his office as soon as I arrived. Upon arriving at National Airport, I had just missed a shuttle and there was a 40 minute wait before the next one. While driving to the airport, I tried to determine why me? Why was I being called before the division president without having a chance to pack an overnite bag? First, I reasoned it had to be something to do with blacks. Secondly, I reasoned that someone in a position to demand answers had created a "panic" situation. Third, I reasoned that the person or persons demanding answers was either IBM's C.E.O., Thomas Watson, or the government. And fourth, the problem,, if it had to do with "Negro's" in IBM, it must concern their almost complete absence in the employee ranks. Feeling the need for some advice, and not having much time, I sped toward the nearest phone booth and called my friend and best man at my wedding, who was now managing editor of the Washington Edition of the Afro American Newspaper. Luckily, he was in, and after explaining my problem,, received one of the fastest and most complete lectures ever delivered on "why businesses were not hiring qualified Negro's, why many Negro's gave up trying and what has to be done. That friend was Charles "chuck" Stone, who went on to become a noted columnist and lecturer and was the "Jackie Robinson" in opening many doors for blacks in the communications media.

Upon arriving at the headquarters building in New York City, I was immediately escorted to Gordon Moodies office. Besides Moodie, the director of Personnel was present, It was after 6:00pm and most employee's had left for the day. Gordon

Moodie opened up the meeting by explaining that IBM has been very unsuccessful in recruiting Negroes and thought that perhaps I could provide some answers.I replied by asking if IBM had sought the assistance of the Urban League and the NAACP. At this point the director of Personnel jumped in and said that these were radical and reactionary organizations that IBM didn't wish to be associated with. Sensing my displeasure, Gordon Moodie immediately jumped in and stated that he was wrong in his description and that they may be "revolutionary" in their objectives, but not reactionary. The director of personnel, after that outburst, had little to offer for the remainder of the meeting. I then asked Gordon Moodie what they wanted to hear, Did they want to hear opinions that would bring smiles to their faces and would accomplish nothing, or did they want to hear the facts, as I see them, ones that would leave them extremely upset and probably cause some ulcers in the executive ranks? But if they faced the issues and accepted with plans to change past practices, it could bring fruitful results. Gordon's reply was to "upset me". The key point that I made was that IBM, like practically all major corporations, had a lousy image in the black community. After 13 years in the business, I was able to describe what any black applicant faced when applying for any "white collar' position in IBM. Gordon interrupted by stating that the reason many managers are giving for not hiring blacks, is that they don't apply. My reply was that if you reversed chairs, lived in a society that was dominated by black businesses that only hired blacks, and discovered that anytime you or any other white applied for a job, you were kicked out the door,unless you were a complete fool or had a brass plated rear end, you would stop applying. I also stated that since the presidents fair employment practices program was enacted and agreed to by most corporations, the pass word in industry became, CYA, or "cover your ass". I stated that IBM was no different. They felt they were covering theirs by hiring three, including me. So when asked if they had any, they could point to us and say "sure, we have three of them".

Gordon then asked me if I would attend a meeting being held in White Plains, New York the next afternoon. He wanted me to discuss my ideas at this meeting. A reservation was made for me to stay at the Summit Hotel and a Mr. Walter Noe would arrange to take me to White Plains. Having arrived in New York with no change of clothes or toilet acceessories, I purchased what was needed before checking in at the Summit. The reason I mention this is, because of company rules, the auditor refused to approve these expenses. When I offered to send him the socks, underwear, shirt and razor (non-electric), that I purchased,he approved my expenses.   So here I am, at a restaurant in mid'manhattan, waiting for our lunch to be served, with Walter Noe on his third martini and I on my third cup of coffee. Two over my quota, so I could remain highly attentive while "Walt spilled the beans".A former private during W.W.II. with eyes and ears wide open, being let in on corporate secrets. I interrupted Walt to ask "Aren't you ready for another martini?"

As Walt continued to quench his thirst, he said "Lionel, here you are a Negro, with no rank in the corporation, suddenly being called on to address a room full of corporate vice presidents. I imagine you're wondering what the hell is going on and why you? I know you were told that IBM is trying to find the reasons why Negro's don't apply for employment at IBM, and you were brought in to possibly provide some answers.   Well that's a bunch of horseshit. You were brought in because Tom Watson (the CEO) is all over their asses, just like Lyndon Johnson was all over Tom's the other day.." Walt continued.. "You see, a couple of days ago, a young black kid applied for a job at our Arlington, Virginia office. They immediatedly tested him, told him he flunked and then escorted him to the door. Within two hours, Lyndon Johnson, who as Vice President, had as one of his responsibilities, the Presidents "Plans for Progress Program", where corporations signed on, pledging to bring Negro's into the fold, was relating to this incident as he raked Watson over the hot coals. You see, Lionel, IBM signed that pledge years ago, and the Vice president wanted to know what IBM had accomplished. After Watson said he would get back to him after gathering the figures, all the division presidents and top corporate officers were ordered to immediately report their progress since the pledge was signed. You've been around for

5

13 years, so I don't have to tell you what the figures were. You know what pissed Tom Watson Jr. off more than anything else? Not the fact that no programs were in place and the same old practices continued. What pissed him off was that this was the first time a Watson sent out a directive and it was completely ignored. In other words, management viewed it as a cya (cover your ass) directive that Watson sent out for his own benefit." Walt continued... "Can you imagine the response from Johnson when Watson told him they hadn't done a damn thing? Lionel, they were frantic. Watson was boiling and no one could provide answers or possible solutions that made sense. That's when Gordon Moodie decided to bring you in. And, oh, by the way, Lionel, the lunch is on me," as he whipped out his IBM charge card. In our discussion, Walter treated me as an equal and I could sense that this was going to be a good relationship. Walt, now deceased, earned my respect for his honesty and directness in our relationship.

So here I am, in a chauffeured limousine with Walt, being driven to IBM's Data Processing Headquarters in White Plains, New York. An enlisted man, asked to advise a room full of generals who for the most part are frustrated because they're being ordered to venture into areas that they have always ignored and are totally unfamiliar to them. Walt was sitting beside me, sometimes nodding during the long trip to White Plains and perhaps wondering how much I could keep confidential. If Walt's spirit is around, this is to let you know its the first revelation. This gave me time to think, to return to my first meeting with my future mentor and very good friend, Thomas Laster,(also known by his friends as T.G.), and my entry into IBM in 1950 and becoming their first sales representative of color.

CHAPTER II

"FACING THE BARRIERS OF BIG BLUE"

In 1947 President Truman was campaigning for re-election, running against the governor of New York, Thomas Dewey. Serving in five campaigns during World War II with Patton's 3rd Army in the European theatre as a private from 1943 to January 1946, I not only felt that many Europeans were liberated, but in a sense, so was I. After the bitter experience of receiving basic training at Fort Rucker, Alabama and suffocating in the prejudices of the then segregated army and surroundings, I decided it would be best to serve as a private and serve my time. This I did, refusing many offers of promotion. The only exception was during the German breakthrough in December 1944 when a call went out for those qualified, to volunteer to receive a battlefield commission in the infantry. At the time, I was in an ammunition supply unit which was considered non-combatant. When first drafted, I was informed that my test scores qualified me for Office Candidate school, but no offer was made to me or any of the others in my group, a few whose scores were much higher than mine. One was a college professer and another became a New York Supreme court justice. Rejected for a "battlefield commission", I later learned they were only interested in "Negro" enlisted men who were accepted and integrated into combat units until the war ended, and then returned to segregated units.

Upon discharge, I returned to my birthplace, Newark, New Jersey. While attending school and working for the Newark Housing Authority, I learned that the Hoffman Beverage Company, subsidiary of the Pabst Brewing Company, was interested in hiring a "Negro" salesman to work in Harlem, the predominantly black area of the borough of Manhattan. In 1947, working as a salesman for a major corporation, or for that matter any company, was an exceptional opportunity for a black. On

7

paper, many of the other applicants were better qualified, but the Vice President that made the decision selected me because, as he put it, I was harrassing him with phone calls.

Selling Pabst beer and Hoffman Beverages, gave me valuable experience and beneficial contacts. In 1948 an associate of mine introduced me to my future mentor, T. G. Laster. T. G., at the time, was the only black employed by IBM in a "white collar" position. We developed a growing friendship, despite the fact that his position kept him traveling throughout the country.

In 1950, I received a call from C. Udell Turpin. I didn't know Mr. Turpin but he knew of me. Mr. Turpin was a Special Representative with the Remingon Rand Corporation and to my knowledge, he also was the only black in a white collar position. I was informed that Remington Rand was interested in hiring me as a sales representative and would I be interested. I was interviewed by a Vice President, offered a position and informed that I would receive a call in a week to ten days as to my starting date. I gave Pabst my notice, they gave me a great farewell party expressing their regrets that I was leaving, and I sat back and waited for my call from Remington Rand, which didn't come. After ten days, I called the Vice President that interviewed me and inquired as to my starting date. I will never forget his reply: "Mr. Fultz, since our interview the Korean War broke out and we need a new salesman like we need a hole in the head". At first I couldn't believe what I heard. At the time, Remington Rand was a major corporation soon to be headed by General Douglas Mac Arthur. Fortunately, Pabst wanted me back and tore up my resignation.

Shortly after, T.G. offered me the possibility of being employed by IBM. The road was much smoother. After filing my application, I was given a starting date and training schedule. I would be working at IBM's World Headquarters in New York City, attending morning classes in "unit record equipment" and then operating the equipment and wiring control panels in the afternoon at their Service Bureau.

Learning how to wire control panels and feeding information into machines with punched cards was challenging and illuminating, allowing me to envision great opportunities for anyone fortunate enough to be in this field. After six months, my classroom studies had ended and my duties in the service bureau became "working" the equipment, rather than learning different applications. Thus arose my first confrontation with IBM management.

To better explain the situation I was in, let me familiarize you with my mentor and friend at the time, Thomas G. Laster, or as he wished to be called. T.G. T.G. was discharged from the army in 1945 and returned to teaching at Tennesee State University. While in the army, he became familiar with IBM equipment used in testing recruits. As he explained it to me, he was no longer satisfied in his present position and decided to explore the possibility of joining IBM. Considering that the year was 1945 and he was a black man teaching in Tennessee, T.G. had an excellent chance of being admitted to an insane asylum if he announced his intentions. Regardless of the million to one odds against his even getting to 1st base, he wrote a prospectus on how IBM equipment could be used in many black businesses and educational institutions throughout the south. Prospective business that, because of the times, was practically being ignored. He sent it to Thomas J. Watson Sr., founder and Chairman of the Board of IBM. T.G. was invited to New York by Mr. Watson, offered a position as Special Representative, served for 30 years assisting in sales around the country, teaching executive classes in IBM's customer schools. And yet retired with the same title, Special representative. Despite his many accomplishments, T.G., as related to me by him, was never offered a management position by IBM.

Throughout my career, T.G. was a severe critic, mentor and good friend. He was a genius ahead of his time, who had a lot to offer but was feared by his superiors because of his strength and knowledge. So great, it could overwhelm you. Despite IBM's recognized prowess in the business world, they failed to fully utilize a great mind. as was often the case during those times.

I first met T.G. in 1948.. He and his wife, Mildred, also a former teacher at Tennessee State University, were close neighbors. Being close neighbors and having the social graces of southerners, he and Mildred gave me a standing invitation to

9

dinner which I accepted so often that I began complaining about being served leftovers. By this time I was considered part of the family, so Mildred simply ignored me.

Early in 1950, T.G. asked me if I would be interested in working for IBM. He explained that I would have to take extensive training and a 60% reduction in what my present job paid. My present job was in sales so I assumed that I would be training for a sales position. After six months, my classroom training was concluded and nothing seemed to be happening as far as my moving into a sales position. I decided to see my immediate manager, who supervised the service bureau. I came right to the point and asked when I would be moving into a sales position. He wasn't upset but appeared to have a puzzled expression on his face. I guess he thought that I was either crazy or intoxicated. This was the spring of 1951, and IBM not only didn't have any black sales representatives but hiring one was, at that time, not even being considered. The manager asked what gave me the idea that I was being considered for sales. I suggested he look at my employment application, which clearly stated a sales position, and also indicated that I was taking a 60% cut in pay from my previous position.. His expression suddenly changed and replied that he would look into the matter.

From what I later learned, phones started ringing all over the headquarters building. T.G. had gotten me on a temporary payroll and not one of those responsible for my training bothered to inform me that I was not hired to be an IBM sales representative or a permanent employee. At the time, the country was in the thick of the Korean conflict and very little, if any hiring was being done for sales positions. Also, I later learned that there were no sales training classes being held. The next day I was told to report to the office of the Corporate Secretary.

His office was in what was called "the ivory tower". A secretary in the reception area was expecting me, and immediately took me into the office of the corporate secretary. Without going into any detail, he said I was to report to IBM's Chicago-South branch office the next day to begin my new position as a electric typewriter-time equipment sales

10

representative. I thanked him for the opportunity but said that on such a short notice, it would be impossible to get there the next day. He then told me to take an extra day and asked if there was anything else. I told him there was the matter of traveling expenses and getting set up in Chicago. Taking such a deep cut in pay for the last 7 months, caused me to use up most of my savings. He then signed a slip and told me to go down to the cashiers office and they would give me whatever I felt I needed. With this, I turned to leave, thinking what a great company, giving me all this money to get started. That thought lasted for only a split second, however, because before I could close the door, I heard a voice say, "When you arrive in Chicago, file an expense account so you 'll know what you have to pay back for non-business expenses.

T.G., through friends in Chicago, had arranged for me to rent a room with a very nice couple, the Hanners. Mr. Hanners , a chef on the railroad, was nearing retirement. They had a very large apartment in a three flat building on Chicago's south-side. Their apartment occupied the 2nd floor, had three bedrooms and two baths. My bedroom was in the rear of the apartment and I had a private bath. My rent was five dollars a week. It was located on south 51st street, facing Washington Park and a short distance from the University of Chicago.

The Hanners were extremely nice. Their biggest problem was explaining to some of their friends that I wasn't a con man. In fact, one friend, a public school teacher, wanted to give Mrs. Hanners odds on a one hundred dollar bet that I wasn't a sales representative for IBM. One hundred dollars then was worth over one thousand dollars in todays market. Eventually, I met this teacher, showed him by business card, and he still had doubts.

For those not familiar with job opportunities during that era, this may sound crazy. But, to my knowledge, I wasn't aware of any black sales representative, on the streets, selling for any corporation dealing in office products or business equipment in the country. In fact, whenever a black was hired by a major corporation for a white collar position, this was a big news item in the black community. And in those days, such items were

11

very infrequent. I've been reading Jet magazine since it was first published by Johnson Publishing, also the publisher of Ebony magazine. The one section I enjoy reading in Jet is their newlywed section. And not because it shows who got married. What it always lists is the profession and jobs of the bride and groom. Having known many black professionals who could only earn a living by taking jobs far below their qualifications, i.e.: a dentist working for a small black newspaper, a lawyer working as a redcap, a chemist working as a porter...As most from my era know, the best jobs available for blacks was working on the railroad as a pullman car porter or waiter or working in the postal system. Today, in Jet Magazine, the brides and grooms aren't running the fortune 500 companies they're working for, but they are in their professions: "Auditor, chemist, engineer, etc. So when I say that many blacks wanted to see proof when informed that I was an IBM sales representative, I can understand why.

At this moment, in the spring of 1951, I only had my foot in the door. I was certain that many in a position of power in IBM, felt hiring a black as a sales representative was a mistake and were convinced that person would fail.. It had nothing to do with me, personally, because just a handful of people had met me. In a nutshell, their feeling, no matter who was hired, was that no black could make it. So as I started my new position in IBM's Chicago-South office, I knew it would be a very tough ordeal to survive, but what I wasn't prepared for was "dirty tricks". And this was in 1951, over 20 years before the Watergate era, when the phrase "dirty tricks " became famous. So here I am, entering offices that appeared to be a former supermarket but now occupied by the IBM-South branch office. Things happened so fast in New York, that they gave me no name of who to report to, just the branch manager. The receptionist seemed puzzled when I identified myself as a transfer employee from New York. Probably because they already had a janitor and he was still employed. Lucky for me, Alexander Bell invented the phone, because no one in New York notified Chicago that I was being assigned to their office. My first impression was that they thought someone was playing games and expected that after a phone call and a few "Caught You", the practical joke would be over and I would be shown the door. The managers offices were open with glass partitions and you could easily observe what was going on. After a few phone calls and a meeting of several people in the corner office, the branch manager finally came out to greet me. His name was Joe Sweeney, who, from his age, was a veteran in the business. Joe Sweeney managed the Electric Accounting Machine business, the forerunner of data processing and solid state computers. IBM's first solid state computer, the RAMAC was still in the development stage. As branch manager, Joe Sweeney had overall responsibility for the office and a dotted line repsonsibiliy for the other two product sales groups, electric typewriters and time equipment. If you divided Chicago into four quarters:, roughly, the south office covered the southeast quarter. In business potential, the south office was the smallest branch in Chicago. The elecric accounting machine group had nine sales representatives, time equipment, two, and my group, electric typewriters, four. The four included me and my manager, who also covered a territory. All sales representatives carried quota, but due to the Korean war, no commissions were paid . Everyone was on a salary. My manager gave me a couple of days to get settled, probably because he seemed confused as to what he was supposed to do with me. The only black employee in the branch was Percy Robinson, who besides pushing fifty was also pushing a broom. I didn't know Percy's educational background but from our conversations it was obvious to me that he was qualified to do better things. Percy kept to himself most of the time. Doing his job and only speaking when spoken to. However, he did speak to me whenever he felt we weren't being observed. Percy occasionally would find it necessary to polish or clean up in the vicinity of the managers offices when meetings were going on. Since the offices weren't entirely enclosed, he would "accidentally" hear tidbits of information that may have been private.

Not long after my arrival, he said he couldn't keep from informing me of one discussion where a manager predicted that I would be gone in thirty to sixty days. I also was not given any sales training. Fortunately, one sales representative, Steve Krask, who was nearing retirement, offered to help me get started. It was far from sales training, but he did offer his help whenever possible.

When I was given my first territory agreement, I could see why they predicted 30 to 60 days. The territory covered an area that was 100% black and 95% residential. It also included restrictions: "I could not call on any business that was white owned or managed." It excluded all educational and hospital institutions that were white managed,, I was even restricted from selling to a small family shoe store if it was white owned. This left me four small black owned and managed insurance companies,barber shops, (black of course), black lawyers and doctors and other small businesses providing they were black owned. All this was in writing which I had to sign. I asked for but could never get a copy of that agreement. The copy wouldn't have done me any good in those days since "fair employment practices" was not part of the vocabulary in the United States.

It was obvious to me that this terrritory could not sustain a quota, even if you got every typewriter that was purchased. However, if I questioned the fairness, I had no facts or figures to prove my case, since I was totally unfamiliar with the area. So I decided to hold back my objections until I completely covered the area. This I started to do, keeping a daily record of every call, who I spoke with and the results.

One of my earliest calls was to the Supreme Life Insurance Company, (owned and managed by blacks). They used IBM electric accounting machines but someone apparently wasn't familiar with the account, as events proved. I asked to speak to the office manager, but she referred me to the controller who had asked that I be directed to her if I called. Being escorted to the controllers office, I couldn't figure out how she knew of me, since there was absolutely no public announcement of my being with IBM. The controller, a very distinguished looking woman with great presense, smiled and asked me to have a seat. She said that she received a call informing her that their new sales representative, some Amos and Andy character, would soon be calling on their company, and they just wanted to forewarn her.

14

This was the first of many "dirty tricks" to follow. This and other actions only strengthened my determination to wade it out.

A few months after I first arrived in Chicago, there was a lot of commotion around the office. Most of the sales representatives were on their way out to the field, but I was asked to stay. It wasn't long before a tall, pre-maturely gray haired, well-dressed man came into the office. I recognized him as T.J. Watson Jr., recently installed as president of the corporation and heir apparent to his father, the Chairman of the board. I later learned that he had been visiting with the regional manager, Gordon Smith, and decided to visit our office. Just one guess as to why. Within a few minutes, I was called into the branch managers office. Mr. Watson's questions were mostly personal, "Are you married?" "Do you plan on getting married soon?" "When?" etc. No, he didn't ask for my autograph or have a picture taken with me. I have no idea of the purpose of the visit other than to see and observe me. It was no meeting because there was no two way discussion of anything of substance.

For the next ten months I called on doctors, lawyers, real estate offices, dress shops, restaurants,barber shops...any place where there was a possibility of selling time equipment or electric typewriters..(I still hadn't been enrolled in sales school}. During this period most businesses were using manual typewriters that cost less than $100.00. The least expensive IBM Electric was $370.00. Considering the territory, I did manage to sell a number of typewriters and time equipment to mostly new customers.

Since most businesses were very small and operating on a shoestring, I found a way to determine which businesses might possibly afford a $400. electric typewriter. Back then, air conditioning wasn't a standard item in small struggling businesses. So I would look for air conditiners sticking out the window. Since air conditioners were very expensive back then, I reasoned that they might be able to afford an electric typewriter. That was my initial way of qualifying an account. Most couldn't afford the cost but I did make some sales. It taught me to qualify accounts so as not to waste words and time.

A number of black professionals were so surprised [and elated] to see me in my position, they purchased equipment just to help me out. Just to mention two accounts, Arthur B. Knight Insurance Agency and Dr. T. K. Lawless (a world-renowned dermatologist.) Both of these gentlemen have been deceased for some time but I'll always remember their effort to assist me. As an example, Dr. T. K. Lawless had purchased time equipment and electric typewriters from me. He had IBM equipment throughout his offices. Towards the end of the year, he asked me if I was going to make my quota. When I told him that I may run a little short of quota, he asked if there was anything else I sold besides time equipment and electric typewriters. It so happened that we had just introduced a lectern..Very fancy with all kinds of controls. The story went around that Mr. Watson must have had trouble with a lectern while making a speech, so he had IBM engineers design one to his satisfaction. They were quite expensive and I couldn't imagine what use Dr. Lawless could make of it. However, he insisted on buying one. I later learned that he kept it in his office for six months and then donated it to Dilliard University (a Historic black college) in Louisiana where he served as a trustee.

Mr. Knight ran a very successful insurance agency. He gave me my first order. He was so anxious to help and encourage me, he purchased our most expensive electric typewriter, the Executive. It cost almost $700.00. His secretary did very little typing and he could have gotten along with their present typewriter. John Johnson, Publisher of Ebony and Jet, also went out of his way to give me business, once his company became part of my territory.

Making my quota was an impossibiliy with this territory and my manager, perhaps surprised at what I was selling, did nothing to increase my territory. I had kept a daily record of all my activities and completely covered every possible account in my territory. Considering todays environment, describing actions taken forty five years ago may seem weird, but I'm sure that those blacks who endured the plight of finding a decent job during those years,would understand.

I attended sales school [at long last] during the summer of 1952. The school took place at IBM's new plant in Poughkeepsie, New York. Except for a couple of classmates who had transferred from engineering to sales, all the others (except me, of course) had recently entered the business. I'm happy to say that a few years later the sales school was reorganized and improved greatly. The school I attended, however, was a big waste of time and money. The class was managed by the assistant sales manager of the division. His agenda appeared to be, do anything to keep busy during the morning, go to lunch and then head for the golf course and tennis courts in the afternoon. We had a few guest instructors who were in upper level management. We received great pep talks but learned nothing regarding selling our products.

Towards the end of the second, and thank god, the last week, we had to gather with a large crowd in front of the plant for dedication proceedings. Tom Watson Sr., and other top officials were seated on the rostrum. For entertainment there were two famous stars from the Metropolitan Opera, Ponzell and a male baritone whose name I can't recall. It was an extremely hot and sunny day. The temperature must have been 105 in the shade, and we were in the sun in our uniforms; suits, white shirts and striped ties..While we were burning up, Mr. Watson was sitting there, vest and everything, as cool as a cucumber. Taking notice of Mr. Watson's obvious comfort despite the heat, one of my suffering classmates leaned over and said that he probably had the engineers build him an air-conditioned suit.

Despite our lack of training, this class probably broke all records considering the number that advanced to high positions in the business. One classmate was promoted within a year, and many others within the next two years. Practically everyone in that class who wanted to go into management got the opportunity in the next 3 or 4 years. Of course, I was not included in those statistics.

My friend, T.G. Laster was still working out of IBM's world headquarters in New York, as a special representative, assisting IBM offices that covered black insurance and educational institutions. We kept in touch, frequently, by phone. T.G. never liked to talk with me over the office phones. If he called during the day, he would ask me to go to a phone booth and call him back at a certain number. Why? The same reason, Percy, the janitor, would never engage me in a conversation if we were being observed. If T.G. was identifying a person who was black, if being observed, he would use the code "club member". Today the word is "brother" and its used openly..

There were many instances in my career when I saw black's penalized or denied promotions because of their close association with other blacks in the company. We weren't in South Africa where there were laws preventing black groups from congregating. But, despite the fact that as a group we had very little power, the fear was in the minds of management.

I was ready to make my move but wasn't exactly sure how to proceed. I called from a phone booth and asked T.G. to call me back.

In 1952, prejudice and discrimination reigned in our society and in Corporate America. There were no sit-ins, civil rights marches or opportunities for blacks in corporate America, regardless of their qualifications. The handful of blacks, including myself, who were employed in other than menial positions, knew we were being used as "window dressing". If a company was criticized for discriminating against blacks, they could prove they had one. Realistically, prejudices were so deep-rooted in our society, that corporate America didn't worry about being criticized about their policies because there were few signs that anyone cared. To protect my position or gain a step, it was always imperative that I find someone who might care if I got my message across.

In 1952 IBM was much smaller than its present size. Thomas J. Watson Sr., Chairman of the Board was talking about the possibility of someday reaching One billion in sales. The company was split up in three regions, east, midwest and west, with a regional manager in charge of all operations. These regional managers were very powerful and all product divisions reported to them.

The regional manager for the midwest was Gordon Smith, and he was based in Chicago. I knew nothing of Gordon Smith

18

but T.G. was very familiar with him. He said that Gordon's parents were missionaries in China and from what he knew about him, was fairly open minded. He recommended that I go to Gordon Smith. I knew my job rested on whether Gordon Smith will care if I got my message across. Having recently married and with my wife expecting our first child, I knew there was a risk of being thrown to the wolves at a time when my personal responsibilities were increasing. Despite the consequences, someone had to make the first move and I was in the position to do it. I decided to throw the dice.

The next morning I went in to see my manager, who really hadn't shown any interest in what I was doing. I told him that I had covered all potential prospects in the territory, that there wasn't enough for me to do and therefore I needed more accounts to call on. I showed him all my records, which he was aware of since I copied him every week. But I wasn't surprised when he rejected my request. So I went out to my desk and started reading the New York Times. After a few minutes, he came to my desk and asked why I wasn't out in the territory. I reminded him that there wasn't enough to do. He then replied that I couldn't stay in the office and walked away. I then picked up the phone and called Gordon Smith's office.

When he answered, I identified myself and said I had a serious problem and would like to see him. He told me to be in his office at 8:30 the next morning. The quick appointment caught me by surprise but I later learned that he was aware of my problems and wasn't surprised to get my call.

I arrived at 8:00 and Gordon arrived soon after. He had also asked my manager and his boss, Gordon Moodie, to be there. (Gordon Moodie managed typewriter sales in the region and reported to Gordon Smith). Gordon Smith opened the meeting by simply stating: "Lionel, you asked for the meeting, what's the problem?"

I told Gordon that when I came to IBM, I expected to be given a fair chance to succeed or fail. No more or no less than any other new sales representative. I then described my terriory, giving him all the statistics, and then stating that other new representatives were given territories that at least had the

19

potential for business. As for my territory, it did not have the potential, and from my records, this had been proven. He then turned to my manager and asked why I wasn't given a fair territory.

My manager's answer couldn't have been worse to someone with the background of Gordon Smith. His reply was that the customers wouldn't accept me, in fact I might even be in danger. To make his point he cited a very recent race riot in Cicero, Illinois, a suburb of Chicago, mostly a blue collar community. An apartment was rented to the wife of a black couple who was very fair and thought to be white. When she moved in with her husband, this lit the fuse. Cicero, to this day, has always been a powder keg. It initially made its reputation as being the operations headquarters for Al Capone. Gordon Smith turned towards me and asked what was my reply to my manager's concerns. I could see that he was irritated by my manager's reply but wanted me to respond.

I asked Gordon if the people in Cicero who were rioting had to be described by their occupation, where would they be working? In the front office or in the warehouse or loading docks? I said that the people we normally deal with aren't working on the loading docks, they're in the front office. And even though I'm not a native of this area, I doubt whether they live in Cicero or were participating in the riot. Gordon Smith said only two words: "you're right". He then turned to my mnager and told him to give me a fair territory.

This marked my initial "Open Door" in IBM. "Open Door" is an IBM policy that allows any employee to go to their managers manager if they feel they've been treated unfairly. Up until my retirement, if records are kept, I may have the record for "open door" hearings during my career with IBM. Three times to the Chairman of the Board, three times to the president of my division and over 10 times all together. I always won my case but I soon learned that I was being targeted and stayed on the "S" list. And that doesn't mean sugar.

Following Gordon Smith's instructions, my manager gave me additonal territory. By my estimate, it was approximately 60% of what the previous salesman was covering. And this salesman was asked to resign because he wasn't making his quota. Geographically, it expanded my present territory around 20%, which , as previously noted, was most of the residential area housing blacks on the south side of Chicago. This also became my personal experience with the practice of gerrymandering. It was so designed that it excluded the major meat packing company's, including Swift and Armour, the University of Chicago (that, geographically was located in the middle of my territory and was one of the biggest accounts), and the headquarters of the Fifth Army, an account that placed an order so large, not long after, that the sales representative covering the account was the second highest in sales in the country. Though Gordon Smith's instructions weren't carried out to the letter, the territory was a big improvement over what I had before. Looking back, perhaps I should have protested and gone back to Gordon Smith. At the time, though, I didn't feel I was in a position of strength or certain as to how far I could go in seeking help. When I made the appointment to see Gordon Smith, considering the times and not knowing Gordon Smith, I felt the odds were shaky. Also, I couldn't count on my manager repeating himself when he characterized street rioters in the same vein as the people we call on in the front offices. From Gordon Smith's reaction to my reply, *I knew I scored the winning run for that game. I couldn't be certain, at the time, how far Gordon Smith would go in backing me up. In simple words, before, the water was almost frozen and if I jumped in, there was no way I could reach shore. With this expanded territory, the water was still pretty cold, but I felt I had a chance of making it. Around 1941, I happened to be in the company of the great "world class" track and field athelete, John Borican. who held many world records at the time. I've always remembered the reply to my question as to how he achieved so many records. He said that he had the skills, but being a Negro meant that the stick was always higher when he high jumped, the fault line always closer to his last step when he jumped and the timer always faster when he ran. Having to jump higher, take off further from the fault line and run faster to qualify gave him the incentive to do more than his best. In a few memorable words*

21

that I always remembered, he was telling me that the biggest mistake I could make is to operate as if the rules were the same for me. Or, if you want to get credit for jumping six feet, you better jump six and a half feet.

CHAPTER III

"IN THE TRENCHES"

In 1952, a black sales representative was hired to work in IBM's Detroit office. John Lewis was from Atlanta, Georgia and I was told had received several degrees from Ivy League schools.

Not long after assuming a sales territory in Detroit, I learned that John had a conflict with the regional manager in the Detroit area and was transferred to our New York City office soon after. After Gordon Smith left our region for a position in headquarters, one of the initial acts of the new regional manager was to pass out confederate flags to all the branch managers so that the salesmen could display them on their desk. This I refused to do. T. G. informed me that this was the same regional manager that John Lewis had a run-in with. Fortunately John was able to get a transfer instead of being fired. T. G. told me that John's father was a prominent educator in Atlanta who had initially recommended his son to Tom Watson Sr., at a commencement exercise.

During the next three to four years, in the mid-1950's, three additonal sales representatives were hired in our office but no additional black sales representatvies were hired by IBM in the entire country. IBM had two black systems representatives in New York City, both female. Amongst major corporations in America, I knew of one national sales representative with Phillip Morris and two sales representatives hired by Remington Rand during the mid-fifties. From what I learned, only beer, wine and liquor company's and distributors were hiring black sales representatives in metropolitan areas with large black populations.

Despite the purchasing power of a black population of over twelve million, representing billions in sales, Corporate America was only giving back pennies to the black community. Corporate America's image of the blacks acceptance by the white

23

community was such that when Nat King Cole and other black musicians became very popular, initially they would put their names on the record covers but not their pictures. Why? They felt the white public would not buy a record with the picture of a "Negro" on the cover. This was the attitude of Corporate management as I was about to get a territory that had predominantly "white" accounts. Fortunately, I felt different. I felt there were many "Gordon Smith's" out there who would listen if I had a good story to tell.

At the time, during the mid-fifties, I had a positive attitude but cannot confirm that IBM management felt the same about my future..

My manager was promoted to a larger office in Minneapolis in 1954 and was replaced by the former manager of our Hammond,Indiana office, Joe Nocco. Joe grew up in the coal mining area of Pennsylvania, was built like a line tackle and didn't mince his words if he had anything to say. Joe knew he wasn't going much further in the business because he wasn't considered a "team player" or as he put it, an "ass kisser". The word throughout our division during that time and for years to come was that you had to be part of the "Irish Mafia" if you expected to move up in the business. It was an expression that definitely didn't apply to all Irish employees. Years later, one of the most talented managers I ever worked with was Bob Brady, a true Irishman from Boston. The more I recommended him to my boss for promotion, the more resistance I got. You see, Bob was a "wild duck", a term I'll discuss covering another episode. However, in a few words, he wasn't a "yes man". Bob was a great manager, but he would have made a lousy politician if he had to say what people wanted to hear.. Joe Nocco also was very outspoken and knew he didn't have a chance to move up the ranks. From what I learned, he continued to be outspoken in managers meetings.

Soon after Joe arrived, he gave me additional territory and some good accounts. However, the prime Account, 5th army headquarters, which was in my geographic territory, he gave to a newer sales representative. Not long after, this sales representative received the huge order I spoke about. [Such an order was commonly called a "bluebird" from the song "bluebird of happiness" Definition:bluebird = unexpected business}..I wasn't too happy with Joe's decision and he later said he was sorry he didn't give me the account. What may have contributed to his later comments is that Joe had given me an account that this salesman was covering..Soon after, according to Joe, he received a call from the office manager representing this account. He told me that this same salesman, who knew I was taking over the account, called the office manager that he dealt with and told him a Negro representative would be calling on him. The office manager told Joe he didn't want me talking with his people, especially the women, and wanted a different representative. Joe told him that he dealt with me, only, if he wanted to do business with IBM. I never knew whether he called the salesman on the carpet, but I could sense that their relationship was very strained. Needless to say, despite my calls, I never received any business. Here was a person, managing the office of a large international corporation, whose products were not only sold in black communities but in third world countries whose citizens also would most likely be objectionable to this company's manager. Despite the fact that we had never met, he refused to see me. After several calls without a meeting, I made better use of my time.

During the mid-fifties, the same attitude most likely prevailed in their headquarters. At the time, I was receiving business from firms that had no black employee's, except those in maintenance jobs. Fortunately, most of those I dealt with gave me the opportunity to disprove any derogatory images that may have prevailed in their minds.

If you attained 100% of quota for the year, you qualified for IBM's one hundred percent club. It usually met the following year in spring or early summer. The first club I attended was in Cleveland, Ohio in 1953. Upon arriving at the hotel, a committee greeted me, took me aside and said that they always put two to a room, but not knowing who would object to staying with me, I was being given a private room. This policy continued for years. I was the only one, including managers, that always had a private room. Before arriving in Cleveland, I called a friend who I used to work with while wih Pabst. The first night there, he and his wife came by to pick me up. While he was parked outside, she came in to get me. I was waiting in the lobby, and we walked out together where her husband was waiting. What I didn't realize, is that many eyes were observing me in the lobby. I found out why the next morning. The three of us went out to dinner and then visited a small club where my favorite singer, Carmen McRae was singing. They dropped me off around 12:30am and I put a wake-up call in for 7:00am. However, I woke up, through habit, at 6:15 and jumped into the shower. After a few minutes, I heard all this banging on the door. I thought perhaps there was a fire or some disturbance. The person hollering said he was the house detective and to open the door. I let him in and he walked right by me, looked in the bathroom, under the bed and in the closet. He didn't apologize but simply said that they received a report that I had a woman in the room. If I had, IBM would have fired me on the spot. This was another reason why, in later years when new black representatives were entering the business and they called me for advice, the first piece of advise was, "no matter who or how many you see breaking a rule without being reprimanded, don't assume that because your wearing a white shirt, dark suit and a striped tie, you're in the same boat. Try it and you're in great danger of being blown out of the water". Later,I will cover a "case in point" when a good friend in the business almost wrecked his career doing "what everybody else did". He forgot that he wasn't being judged "like everybody else".

Two years later, in 1955, the club was in Florida at the fabulous Fontainbleu hotel in Miami Beach. This was really a problem for IBM. The committee asked if I would avoid going to the pool or beach. The restaurant was ok but be careful if you go to any clubs outside the hotel. Of course, I still had a private room.[From 1965 on, things started opening up in Miami]. The first club where I was assigned a roommate took place in Denver, Colorado. Many incidents happened at this club that are worth mentioning.

Despite IBM's great public image, the company had it's problems. The first incident happened in the lobby of the hotel where all the convention activities were being held. Despite IBM's strict rules regarding drinking on the job, this did not apply off the job. Not being much of a drinker, I never knew a single individual could drink so much until I began circulating around my cohorts after meetings. [While attending management school, some years later, a company psychiatrist, during his lecture, said there were over 3000 IBM managers who were in special programs because of their drinking.]

According to the story that circulated around the hotel, Wis Miller, President of the Division and a IBM Corporate Vice President, was standing in the lobby with a group of wide eyed young IBM salesmen circling him. As was described to me, Wis was on his throne and looked everything like the supreme ruler surrounded by his adoring subjects, when an old time salesman, who obviously knew Wis for years, came staggering up to the group and, as related to me, screamed in a drunken voice: "Wis, you old son of a bitch, what kind of bullshit are you throwing around to these young assholes, and on and on." They said he was dead-drunk, but that didn't prevent him from getting the axe. They immediately closed the bar to all IBM'ers.

Soon after that I got involved in an awkward situation. The first evening I was in my room preparing to go to dinner when my phone rang. I picked up the phone: "Mr. Fultz, I'm with the Denver Press and I was given your name". Must be a joke,I thought,so I went along with it. "Yes, what can I do for you?" "Well, I was told you would know what Wis Miller, the division president, is going to talk about at the dinner tomorrow night" ...So I went along, assuming someone was playing a joke on me. "Why certainly, I'd be glad to"..So I rambled on as to how there's going to be a big reorganization of the division, heads were going to fly. etc. etc...After a few minutes, he finally interrupted me and asked: "Why is he making such big changes?" and I replied, "because I recommended it, in fact I'm to become the executive vice president of the division." For a few seconds, I heard nothing on the other end of the line. Then he asked, "you mean to tell me your going from his speechwriter to the #2 position?" I took a deep gulp and asked, "Did you ask to speak with Fultz, spelled F U L T Z?" he answered "Yes,

27

you're George Fultz, aren't you? For the next couple of minutes I explained how IBM'ers are always playing jokes on each other, and apologized for misleading him. Explaining that the operator mistakenly gave him the wrong room. Fortunately for me, the reporter had a better story, but didn't know it. His readers would have enjoyed a good laugh. He only told the story to the speechwriter, George Fultz. I met George in the lobby the next day, He said the story made his day.

The next incident was almost a catastrophe. After I was declared non-contagious and given a roommate who appeared to be a very nice and typical IBM salesman, intelligent, conservative in appearance and the graces of a true gentleman. He was from a small town in the southwest, married with children. That's the only information I'll provide, and you'll understand why after hearing the story. After that initial meeting when we checked in, he disappeared. The convention lasted four days. I didn't see him at any of the meetings, breakfasts, lunches or dinners. Word had gotten around that some salesmen had been ripped off by prostitutes, and I was hoping that it didn't include him.

It's the last day of the convention. The schedule is breakfast, a meeting until noon, lunch..then everyone takes off for their destinations. After lunch, I returned to my room. His suitcase and all his clothes hadn't been touched since his arrival. I decided to pack my bag and take a shower. If he didn't show up by the time I checked out,I intended to notify the convention committee. Our room was on the tenth floor facing the street. What was unusual about the room was this huge glass window running from just above the floor, almost to the ceiling. I was sure it was secure but I still didn't lean on it. I was in the shower about two minutes when I suddenly heard a sound as if someone was crashing through the door. Since no one else was in the room, I had the bathroom door open. The next thing I knew, someone with a beard, fully clothed, moaning and not too intelligible, had jumped into the shower. From the voice, I recognized my roommate. He stunk like a condemned distillery. I immediate got out of the bathroom and started drying myself. He kept mumbling that he had to get to the airport and meet his wife.   After a few minutes he came stumbling out of the bathroom, soaking wet, in his birthsuit. He was stumbling so fast he couldn't hold his balance, and before I could do anything, he crashed into the large window.   Thankfully, it shook but didn't break. I could see the headlines in the local Press if he went through the window. "Drunken, naked IBM salesman kills himself by taking a running jump through a window," with a picture on the front page showing, not a typical IBM salesman but what looks like a bum with a beard."

I started filling my roommate up with coffee, put him under an ice cold shower and got him to shave. What was a miracle was how quick he came around. When he was able to talk, he said that he didn't want to leave me with the wrong impression. He said he has a very nice family and lives in a very nice town, but to quote him, "if you fart, everyone knows it". He said that the only time he gets to let his hair down is when he leaves town for a meeting. He apologized and said he must have been on a "drunken binge" since he left the hotel. His clothes were so ragged, he threw them away. I saw him at the airport later that afternoon. All the traces of his binge were gone and, from all appearances, he was once again the "true blue" IBM salesman.

Tom Watson Jr., Chairman of the Board, who took over from his father a few years back and from all reports was mainly responsible for successfully ushering IBM into the computer age, came to the dinner to give the keynote speech. All agreed that it was the greatest speech he ever gave.   It was called "the wild duck" speech. The essence of the speech was that ducks always fly in a uniform way. Once in a while, however, a wild duck flies out of position and doesn't follow the crowd. Watson said that if IBM was to continue to lead, we need "wild ducks". "Wild ducks" that are ready to risk being shot down, by not following others if they feel its not the best way. "He continued: "the risk is great because you're frequently flying alone, but its necessary that we have some ready to sacrifice their careers to alert us that we may be flying in the wrong direction."

Years later,when I retired, my friends in IBM gave me a plaque with a brass wild duck on it. I've been wounded many times, but never shot down. I don't know whether I deserved the tribute, but I won't give it back.

The time is the early fifty's, Eisenhower is president and the last time I worked for him, [as a private in the European theatre of operations, he demonstrated no inclination to improve the lot for me or my black comrades in the then segregated army. During the German breakthrough in the winter of 1944-45, many infantry units were integrated because of the crises. They remained that way during the advance through Germany. As soon as the Germans surrendered, the high command ordered the units re-segregated and the blacks were sent back to segregated units. My long time friend and fellow draftee, retired New York State Supreme Court Justice Bruce McM. Wright, was one of those volunteers. I agreed to volunteer if given a battlefield commission, but was told there was no need for black leaders, (especially if I would be leading a platoon that included white troops.) After twelve years with IBM, my goal of leading a "platoon" in this company will never bear fruit unless I "shake the tree", and the time is approaching for me to do just that.

It is now 1962 and most of those in my 1952 sales class who sought management positions, have been managers for years. Remembering the German breakthrough and the crisis that followed, I often thought; "will it take a crisis in IBM for me to gain the opportunity to move into management?". I didn't realize it then, but the answer turned out to be "yes". When I asked my regional manager about the possibility of promotion, his reply was that was something they never considered or even thought of since I was a Negro. For eleven years as a sales representative, I had volumes of experiences that I felt made me well qualified for management, so I shall try to relate only a few significant ones that best reflect my overall experience.

One of the accounts I gained was the Illinois Institute of Technology and their research facility, the Armour Research Foundation. It was a large institution with great potential, but our competitors were enjoying the fruit of their business. The individual I had to deal with was the controller, a true Texan, born and reared, who was astonished when I gave him my card. After my presentation, he said that it was their policy to allow all competitors to bid, so I would get an RPQ [request for price quotation), whenever they needed equipment. It seemed fair. However, when I received a request, it also included specifications that matched the Royal electric typewriter. Royal kept getting the business but I also kept calling on the controller, trying to develop some rapport. What I also did was to send him a "thank You" letter for allowing me to bid, even when I didn't get the business. The break came one day when I was attempting to engage him in conversation other than business. I asked him "Don't you sometimes miss Texas?" His reply was my opening; "Yessuh, especially the black eye peas. My wife is a northerner so I don't get that good ole southern cooking". I then told him if he could get away for lunch tomorrow, I'd take him to a restaurant just 15 minutes away that would make his mouth water.He replied; "Hell, what about today".. I took him to "Vernola's", a restaurant known throughout the black community as having the best blackeye peas, collard greens, candied sweets, hot bisquits, ribs, or you name it, on the south side. My Texas client couldn't stop eating. In fact, Vernola told me that he was there practically everyday during the work week.Now should I claim that due to my superior sales skills, the Armour Research foundation became my best account? At least that's what I told my manager when he asked how I broke the account.

Lyons & Carnahan is a publisher of school text books. I picked up this account when my territory was expanded. This was their headquarters and they occupied most of the block. On my initial visit I took the elevator to the "executive" floor. As I emerged from the elevator, I faced this huge open office with no walls, with several hundred people behind desks.The reception area was right next to the elevator. I also noticed that in the dead center of the entire floor, there was an enclosed office, encircled by glass windows, so that its occupant could observe everything that was happening. Since entering the building, I noticed that even the janitor was white. Practically every white owned business that I called on during those days, had no black white collar workers. Many did have janitors. This one didn't. When I approached the receptionist, practically everyone in that office

31

stopped working. As many would say "you could hear a pin drop". I asked to speak to the office manager and presented my card. From the distance, I saw a man pick up the phone after the receptionist dialed. She hung up and replied that he wouldn't be interested. I also noticed that a gentleman sitting in the enclosed office had also taken notice. I realized that my chances of breaking this account may be zero but I was determined to have them reject me to my face. So, at least once a week, I would go through the same procedure. On the fifth call, just as the receptionist started to dial the office manager, a huge voice came booming out of the enclosed office; "send that boy in here".

The office really got quiet. It was at least 150 ft to the enclosed office, and everyone watched every step I took. As I entered the office, this elderly man, wearing cowboy boots and a white cowboy hat, sat there with his feet on the desk. He immediately told me to sit down, [I guess so I wouldn't be looking down on him.],This was the president of the company, Mr Carnahan, and he was in his early nineties. This placed his birthdate around the end of the civil war. I also noticed a large plaque, designating him an honorary Kentucky Colonel. He asked; "Your a salesman for IBM?". I gave him my card, and replied; "for some time". He wanted to know if people were giving me any business and what kind of reaction I was getting. Before you knew it, the gloves were off. and I asked him if it would be better if I was out there robbing someone. After going back and forth for around 20 minutes, he called the office manager in and said "see that this boy gets some business". I did get some business but I still never noticed whether they at least had a black janitor.

Cortez Peters was the world's fastest typist. He did this using a manual typewriter. Being black, he never got much publicity. However, the Royal typewriter company had him on their payroll as a consultant. Mr. Peter's also owned several business schools in different parts of the country. Being on the Royal payroll, it was impossible for him to purchase IBM electric typewriters. We still had a friendly relationship and I sometmes met with him whenever he visited his Chicago school. In 1961, IBM announced the first single element typewriter, the

Selectric.Mr. Peters really wanted them in his Chicago school. The manager of his Chicago School tried to get his agreement, but I understood the problem. Just before my first promotion, he placed a large order that gave me my years quota by June. He never told me how he did it without jeopardizing his relations with the Royal Typewriter Company.

When my old commander in the European theatre during world war II, Dwight D. Eisenhower, left the presidency, I'm certain that very few blacks, if any, shed tears. I would bet that he was the first commander that enacted orders in a foreign country that prevented black soldiers from entering certain English villages.

Or asked black soldiers to die in integrated units when they were needed in desperate situations, then shipped them back to segregated units when victory was won. Black veterans of World War II didn't expect any help from Ike as president, and they were right. Corporate America's policies towards blacks only made changes that were considered "window dressing."

With the election of John Kennedy, tensions started developing throughout the country. One reason was because long lingering racial problems were not being passed over but were being questioned in public. When you want to change things there is always disagreement. Young black students were looking for change while many who disagreed with them and wished to maintain the status quo (and in many cases with the support of law enforcement officers, including the FBI) attacked and maimed them. But they persisted and many of their goals were achieved.

Most of those who started in the business with me who desired and worked towards management, achieved their goals years ago. I knew there would be barriers to my efforts but had no idea how tortuous and tormenting it would be fighting those barriers. Still, I felt now was the time to "shake the tree".

33

CHAPTER IV

"CONFRONTING THE BARRIER TO MANAGEMENT"

The year was 1962, I was nearing my 12th year in the business, segregation still reigned throughout the country and the hiring of blacks in white collar positions defined as the " window dressing" stage. The government certainly didn't set an example for private industry. The few blacks appointed to high level positions received a lot of publicity that gave some the impression that great inroads were being made in fair employment. When people started to list the people who benefited, the same names were repeated and it didn't take long to cover all of them. In the electric typewriter division, in sales, besides myself, there was John Lewis. John. hired in 1952, two years after I started, like myself, seemed entrenched in New York City as a salesman. I never got to know John very well, but whenever we had the chance to meet, his words seethed with frustration. John felt that his knowledge was being wasted and most of those who were above him were not capable. Why did he stay with IBM? One important reason was, " for the money". More important, there was no place else to go. Despite the student sit-ins, boycotts and pledges by many corporate executives, businesses throughout the country were still holding fast, maintaining the same policies, having a couple of black white collar employee's around to ward off criticism and creating the paperwork to C.Y.A...(cover your ---}. I was having one of my best years since entering the business. Since arriving in the Chicago-South office 11 years ago, no sales representative in our office had been promoted. This, despite the fact that the division was growing at a rapid rate and salesmen from other offices were moving into management. With most of those who were in my 1952 sales class now in management, except for those who preferred to remain in the territory. I knew of no black managers in IBM and definitely none in sales. It was June and I

35

was "salesman of the Month" for our district and about to make my years quota. I got a roll of dimes out of the trunk of my car and called T.G. in New York. He, in turn, gave me a phone booth number to call in ten minutes.

I told T.G. that I was ready to make my move and needed his counsel. T.G. agreed with my decision and warned me; "this move won't be the usual one, where the manager calls and informs you that you were recommended for promotion to management and they're ready to make the annoucement. You'll run into more obstacles than you can imagine. Obstacles where you may have to put your job on the line. The odds are stacked against you, but someone's got to make the first move". If my late friend, T.G. is listening, all I've got to say is' "T. G., as you know, it was worse than what you said, but I would do it all over again."

My manager, Joe Nocco, was promoted to IBM's Chicago-West office several years before. His replacement was not one to ruffle any feathers. It was my feeling that he just wanted to do his job, without any controversy, collect his pay,and go home. I did not want to cause him to have a heart attack, so I decided to use a tack that would take him out of the picture.

After exchanging a few pleasantries when we met, I said: "I know the normal procedure for what I'm about to do is to wait for you to make a move, but I don't want to do that, because it would put the onus on you, and that wouldn't be fair to you. Without going into any detail with you, I want you to call your boss, the District Manager, Jack Blaisdel, and make an appointment for me. If he asks, you can assure him that this visit in no way is to be interpreted as a criticism of your management. But because of my peculiar situation regarding my career in IBM, I think its best that I talk with him". My boss sensed immediately that this was something that he didn't want to be involved in, so he immediately picked up the phone and made the appointment.

As a district manager,Jack Blaisdell was responsible for most of the northern part of the midwest. Jack once described his greatest affliction as being "diarrhea of the mouth". What took ten words, Jack would put in 500 words. This, I must admit, I took advantage of by being a good listener. Having been well schooled in the sales profession, I learned never to say more than was necessary to get the order, for the longer you talked, the greater the chance becomes that you wil say the wrong thing. As with Walter Noe, I learned to respect Jack for his honesty and being straight-forward, not mincing his words. After listening to Jack discuss the business for around twenty minutes, he finally got around to me, and asked what was on my mind. I got immediately to the point; "Jack, I've been out in the territory for eleven years, I've watched the business grow and I've seen many of those I started out with, advance with the company's growth. The question is, "given my performance, why have I not advanced?" Without being naive, you and I both know that the one who can best answer that question is the division president, Gordon Moodie. In order not to put you on the spot regarding company policy, I would like you to make an appointment for me to see Gordon Moodie."

Jack seemed stunned, and for a few seconds,(a long time for him) he said nothing. Then he got going. "I'll be quite honest, Lionel, we frequently list a number of individuals we might think of considering for management. Because you're a Negro, you never entered our thoughts. You were just never thought of as being a manager in this business". Jack went on and on. His words may sound insulting, but at least he was being honest. From his words, and judging from policies within the IBM environment, my being a Negro automatically eliminated me from ever managing people in the company. Jack agreed to make the call, thanked me for coming in and said that I would probably receive a call in a few days. I appreciated Jack because he was being honest and not sugar-coating IBM's policies. (Years later I learned that Jack fought hard to get me back to his region as a branch manager but others obviously thought I wasn't qualified}.

Needless to say, my call , I'm sure, initiated several high level meetings at our division headquarters in New York City. I remained patient. The ball was in their court, and I wasn't certain whether a ball would be returned or a rock. Approximately a week later, I received a call from Blaisdel's office. I was to meet with the manager of the divisions Washington Federal Office, the next afternoon at a motel near Chicago's O'Hare Airport.

The Washington Federal office was nicknamed the "West Point" of our division. The office only handled government accounts and all representatives were on salary, with no bonuses or commissions paid.It was also a "graveyard" for former branch managers who were putting in the necessary time before retirement. All of the younger salesmen promoted to the Washington Federal office had successful years in their offices and were considered as "possible high potential" candidates for higher management in the future. After a one to two year stint, some were promoted out as branch managers and some were sent back to the field in their former position. Realistically, there was no way I was being considered as "high potential". This move, as I was to later learn, was to be the first obstacle course to keep me from becoming a manager.

My meeting with the Federal Office's manager was brief. He said there was a position open and I was being considered among others. From the length of the interview and the questions asked, I felt that the decision had already been made, not by the manager, but by someone much higher, to move me to Washington, D.C.

My promotion was the first of a sales representative in our division from the Chicago-South office since it first opened. Our office had the reputation of being a dead-end. The announcement, obviously, came as a surprise to practically everyone in our branch. After the announcement, it was easy to distinguish between the "sincere congratulations" and the one's whose minds were thinking; "what the hell's going on here?" My father often used to say that you can always identify a "true friend", for they will always invite you to their home to break bread with their family and friends.

In my eleven years in the Chicago-South office, I received only one invitation, and that was to the home of Joe Nocco. Martin Luther King, in later years, said that Chicago was the most segregated city in the country. One of my co-workers from Chicago visited my home with his wife soon after we moved to

Washington. I could sense that he wanted to be a close friend, however, this act never played out while we lived in Chicago. One answer stands out and that could have been their fear of being identified as a friend of blacks, or in the phrase that those who wished to maintain the status quo, "nigger lover".

I was fortunate enough to purchase a home in a very nice community that was gradually turning from white to black. I bought my home from an elderly Jewish couple who were having health probelms and could no longer navigate the stairs. The wife had raised her sons in the house and hated to leave. I must have made some impression, because they lowered the price when I said it was more than I could afford. The copy of the deed, (which I still have), had a "restrictive covenant" and stated that it could not be sold to Jews or Coloreds. This was declared illegal in the famous 1948 "Shelly vs Kramer" Supreme Court decision.

My new co-workers in Washington came from all parts of the country, including the deep south where segregation, discrimination and you name it, was still an onus placed on blacks. To me, the office was more a laboratory, rather than a training facility. It was a place where you were being observed and evaluated. One of the evaluators, in reply to my question as to how they determine whether an individual has the abilities to manage, said it's usually "a gut feeling". A better definition for the "gut feeling" that a person can make it, would be that he's labeled a "G.O.B", or "good ole boy".

I was assigned a number of accounts, including the entire Disrict of Columbia Government, Federal Power Commission, Goddard Space Flight Center, General Accounting Office and the Agricultural Research Center. The District of Columbia government was still being run by a congressional committee. I never met one black individual in a high position, no matter what department I visited. I was told that practically everyone who was in a position to wield power was politically appointed, through a congressman. After meeting and discussing business with some of these politically appointed managers, (none who were black), I soon surmised that their qualifications to do the job were as good as mine would be if I had the responsibility to send a rocket to the moon.

The manager of the Washington federal office was considered on the same level as a District Manager. His assistant was one of the first southern republicans to make a realistic run for office in what the democrats called the "solid south" in the fifties and early sixties. I was told that he came close to becoming the first republican office holder in the "solid south".

The IBM Federal office was divided into three programs with three program managers running them. Two of the program managers were former branch managers who were moving close to retirement. The third was usually a candidate for field management. The prime candidates for eventual promotion were usually the ones who were assigned to give presentations in our meetings, branch office meetings around the country or at division headquarters. Division headquarters presentations put the individual in the spotlight. A good presentation could mean a promotion. We had some great presenters. Many of them could have easily qualified as a TV anchor. The question was, "could they manage and motivate people?" But more important, as I learned, "are they a political animal?" I've seen people advance in our business who were lacking in everything except "how to politic". They fail to make quota, they advance. "They create morale problems, they advance. They make bad marketing decisions, they advance. They fail to develop others, they advance. As they say in business, they know where to put their nose. Whenever I hear of a business going downhill, I often wonder what the answer would be if it was determined as to what top ability brought each executive to their position. As Tom Watson said in his great speech. "We need wild ducks in this business if we're to grow, even though most wild ducks are eventually shot down".

While in Washington I learned by listening. I was taught this lesson by the division's first general manager and president, Wis Miller. I had been in Chicago for a year, had recently married and was due a vacation. I decided to drive to see my parents in Newark, New Jersey. A couple of days after arriving, I went to see my friend, T.G., at IBM's world headquarters. He

40

got tied up in meetings, so I went downstairs to the company cafeteria for lunch. As I was eating my lunch, I felt a hand on my shoulder. It was Wis Miller. He asked what brought me to New York and then asked me to stop by his office before I left. This I did and when I greeted him with: "thanks for inviting me, Mr. Miller", he replied: "you're welcome, have a seat, Mr. Fultz". Jokingly, (I hoped), I replied: "Someone told me that when Mr. Watson starts calling you by your last name, you're on the way out. I hope this doesn't portend a bad omen for me?" His reply was , "You put a hanger on my name, so I put one on yours." At that, I became more relaxed. Suddenly I realized that I was doing most of the talking, perhaps 95% of the talking. Me, a private, monopolizing the conversation with a four star general. When I asked why he wasn't doing any of the talking, his reply, which I've always remembered: "you don't learn talking, you learn listening". So I became a good listener. I listened to my customers and my associates in Chicago, my friends, especially T.G, and some of the older managers in Washington.

Almost a year had passed. There were many promotions. The division was growing fast. Given my time in the office, I was about in the middle of the list..I wasn't given any special assignments or asked to give presentations. It was too soon to yell "fire", but I was beginning to get more concerned about my future. Nothing seemed to be happening, that is until I heard my name paged at the Goddard Space flight center in Maryland.

Chapter V

"LBJ Shakes Big Blue's Tree"

From what Walter Noe told me in 1963, during our luncheon before leaving for our meeting in White Plains, Vice President Lyndon Johnson was living up to his reputation as a "Texas straight shooter", who doesen't harbor or tolerate a bunch of B.S. when pledges aren't kept.

Before moving to Washington, D. C., Attorney William Starke of Chicago, a good friend and my oldest daughter's godfather, asked me to call Hobart Taylor Jr., when I arrived. Hobart Taylor was a trusted aid whose family was a long-time supporter of Vice President Lyndon Johnson. Despite his very busy schedule, Hobart went out of his way to help me get settled in Washington. He also almost caused a panic in my office when he left a message for me to call him at the White House.

After Johnson assumed the presidency, I learned through a friend that he stated that he will make Lincoln look like a piker when it came to improving the lot of blacks. From what Noe told me, his hell-raising call to IBM's C.E.O. was probably one of many similar calls to other C.E.O.'s that the public wasn't aware of. As I was about to learn, his call temporarily shattered the "window dressing" policies of IBM at long last.

Walter Noe began to stir as the limousine pulled up to IBM's Data Processing Headquarters in White Plains, New York. It was around 6;00PM and I was quickly escorted to a large room, which I later learned was occupied by most of the top executives in IBM.

I immediately sensed that some in the room appeared a little agitated. I didn't know how long they had been cooling their heels waiting for me, someone who wasn't even a manager? At this point, I had no idea what my role was to be? Whether I was just going to sit, listen and take notes, or whatever. It didn't take me long to find out.

43

There were approximately forty "high level" executives in the room and one chaired the meeting. In just a few words he said; "Mr. Watson signed a pledge with the government that we would initiate a fair employment practices program that would bring Negroes into the business. Since he signed that pledge and issued a directive to the field, nothing has happened. This meeting was called to determine why nothing has been done and decide what has to be done. Lionel Fultz has been in the business for 12 years and is a representative in the Washington Federal office of the Electric Typewriter division. Gordon Moodie suggested that he may be able to answer some of the problems we've confronted. Lionel". He beckoned me to the front of the room.

I opened my remarks by stating that I wasn't sure I could answer all their questions, but if I did have an answer, they would get it straight, even if it hurt to hear it. If they didn't want a straight and honest answer, then they had the wrong person. At this point, the chair directed me not to hold back. I then asked for questions as to what problems they encountered. The first question was the same one Gordon Moodie asked; "Negroe's don't apply". I repeated the same answer I gave Moodie and leaned heavier on the "image" problem of IBM in the black community. As soon as I finished replying, a Vice president jumped up and said "I've heard all this crap about image before, so this morning I asked my "colored" maid if she feels that IBM has a bad image in her community, and she said no". At that, the chair jumped up, very agitated and shouted, "Why the hell would you make such a dumb-ass statement? Don't bother answering, Lionel". The questions didn't last long, because it became obvious to me that no programs were in place, no effort had been made to hire blacks. In fact, though they wouldn't admit it, no one took Watson's directive seriously. In other words, their feeling, which they certainly wouldn't state in public unless they wanted to go on the unemployment list, was that Mr. Watson issued the directive to cover his ass.

After the questions had depleted, they asked what I thought should be the first step in getting a program started. I replied: "The first thing that has to happen is that all managers that do the hiring have to be convinced that they either hire Negroe's or stand to lose their jobs. The only one that can issue such a directive is the Chairman of the Board, Tom Watson. This can't be done by just a written order. Its got to be done, face to face, with his representative letting everyone know that this time, its serious. I recommended that we use the organizations, already in business throughout the country, such as the NAACP and the Urban League to help the local branches recruit. They could also help provide an entree into the black colleges and universities. But even if all these steps are taken and managers who refuse to hire are not removed, the wrong signal will be sent, which will result in excuses rather than results."

When all questions and the discussion ended, it was suggested that I be used as Tom Watson's messenger. I agreed that I could deliver the message and respond to questions, but a high level executive should be present to affirm Watson's directive. I didn't think the affirmation would be effective if delivered by me. Not being a manager it wouldn't appear realistic that I would be speaking for the Chairman of the Board. There was no objection to my suggestions. The meeting concluded, the chair excused me, and I joined Walter Noe as we headed back to New York City.

The next day I reported to Gordon Moodie and discussed the meeting. He informed me that I would be on special assignment, reporting to the Director of Personnel. Soon after reporting back to Washington, I had to return to New York. They had worked out my agenda. They were scheduling group meetings throughout the country, excluding only the deep south. It was 1963, and corporate felt that conditions were too hostile in those states. The procedure was to set up five meetings a week in different cities. All IBM managers, administrative, sales, factories, etc., in specified areas adjacent to that city. were required to report to the meeting. I and the accompanying executive would arrive in the city the night before, with the host manager being responsible for making all arrangements. I would have breakfast with the host manager at the hotel [where the meetings usually took place] then go directly to the meeting. I was given a packet of airline tickets about one and a half inches thick. I could fly home weekends, but that would be my decision. I had a week to get prepared, which wasn't enough time to make certain arrangements that could help the programs in the cities I visited. Depending on the location, attendance could run from 150 to 600.The meetings could last from 2 to 3 hours. I would be introduced by the host manager, give my talk, answer questions and then turn it over to the executive representing Tom Watson. He would affirm Watson's directives, answer questions and state that they "weren't playing games"

Fortunately, most "host Managers", who were usually regional or district managers, cooperated in setting up the meetings. However, a few either thought games were still being played or felt so strongly against the hiring of blacks, that they didn't cooperate. In Chicago and San Francisco, the Data Processing Division managers didn't attend. In one city, the host manager set me up in what is commonly called a "fleabag hotel". I simply picked up my bags, caught a cab to the district managers office and informed them that I would be taking the first plane to New York if suitable accommodations weren't available. The excuse was that there was a big convention in town but after my threat to return to New York, suitable accommondations were found.

The group meetings of all area managers usually ended by noon. My flight schedule to the next city was usually around 5:00 PM. After lunch, this usually gave me around three hours to visit local contacts in the black community that could help our program. Once my credibility with the local contact was established, I not only received their cooperation but frequently learned why no progress in hiring blacks was being made by the local IBM office.

In one instance, I stopped by the Electric Typewriter division managers office in Boston, at his request. As he cleaned his pipe, I listened to how "they scraped the bottom of the barrel, trying to find qualified Negro applicants, to no avail." To make his point, they had an applicant in the office whom they were interviewing, and would I mind talking to him. The applicant they presented to me just sat there without talking. He looked as if he just came in after unloading a garbage truck. It was so obviously a set-up, that either they misjudged me or this was their way of telling IBM what they could do with their program.

Before arriving in Boston I had been given the name of the leader of a civil rights activist group. I left the district managers office to meet this individual for lunch. He was a young black, about 30 years old, very intelligent and strong. He also was very suspicious of me, even though I had a good recommendation from an acquaintance.. Not until I told him that I felt IBM had some serious problems in Boston, did he start to loosen up. He told me that I had no idea how serious the problems were. In fact, the very next morning, the activist group planned to throw a picket line around the IBM building that I had just left. As he explained recent events, what followed illustrates one of the many reasons why black applicants wouldn't apply at IBM.:

"We sent several highly qualified applicants to IBM seeking a job in field engineering. In every case, they were told they failed the written test and therefore weren't qualified. The last applicant we sent wasn't qualified but had a "photographic memory". He failed the test but brought back all the questions. We determined all the answers to the questions, drilled an applicant on the test, and sent him to IBM . Guess what? He was given exactly the same test, gave all the correct answers and was told that he failed. That's why we will be picketing the IBM office everyday, starting tomorrow morning."

At the conclusion of our meeting, I made no promises, but asked if he would be available the rest of the day. He also assured me that he was prepared to state what compliances they expected from IBM before they would call off their picketing. As quickly as possible, I got to the nearest phone booth and was able to reach Walter Noe. I suggested that he relate my information to both Gordon Moodie and the Director of Personnel. From what I knew of Walter, I would bet that he probably tipped off his corporate contacts. Needless to say, things moved quickly. There was no picket line and Boston's "Plans for Progress", I'm certain, got off to a fast start.

My visit to St. Louis was in sharp contrast to the one in Boston. The branch manager for the electric typewriter division in St. Louis was Ship Atwater. He also asked me to stop by after the "big tent" meeting in the morning. Ship said that he hadn't yet hired a black salesman but had just interviewed an army captain in the airborne who really caught his attention. I asked "If you felt he was that great, why didn't you make him an offer?" Ship said that he didn't want to make a mistake and the reason he hesitated is because "he talks differently". I asked "What does he talk like? Ship was hesitating and I could see he was trying to avoid saying the wrong thing. He finally replied, "Well, he talks like he's from the ghetto. I started to ask him, which one, the Italian, Jewish, Polish. etc., but I sensed he was looking for my support if he did make an offer. So I simply replied that if that's where he's from, what's he supposed to sound like? Ship agreed and he did hire the Captain, whose name he didn't mention.

This captain, whose name is Earl Wilson, became, in my opinion, one of the most successful Afro-Americans that IBM employed, not in terms of rank, but what he accomplished for IBM. What does any successful business do with an individual who was national manager of the year, given the highest performance rating, "outstanding", for ten successive years and won numerous awards for his outstanding contributions to the business? Move him into a high executive position so his talents could benefit a larger area of the business? It's sad to say that Earl Wilson was frozen in a middle management position. Being honest and straight forward, when asked, Earl always denoted what he felt was best for the business, not what his superiors may have wanted to hear. Earl Wilson is now retired from IBM and his career demonstrates how IBM and other corporations let tremendous talent slip through their fingers. To better understand how Corporate America often judges Afro-Americans not by performance but by race, I've included a later chapter on Earl Wilson's career with and after IBM, which will further amplify my conclusions.

I was traveling for almost three months, returning home every other weekend. After each meeting I would dictate a belt, giving a narrative of the meeting and mail it to New York.

After it was transcribed, Walter Noe told me it went to division presidents and the chairman's office.

IBM got a head start in recruiting at black colleges. This enabled them to hire what I considered "the cream of the crop".

From my observation, some extremely talented people, many of whom would never be satisfied if not given the opportunity to use all their talents and advance. In my memorandums I warned that if the time came when some of these individuals were prevented from advancing because they were not aligned with the top decision makers, they would leave. At one point, some years later, the Xerox corporation alone had four of these individuals, who were hired and trained by IBM, but left when they realized a "Negro" could advance only to a certain level. They eventually became Vice Presidents with Xerox. One, who was told he would never become a district manager with IBM, resigned and advanced to Division President with Xerox. It's like the Dodger's developing Jackie Robinson and Roy Campanella on their farm team into aces and then letting them go to the Yankee's. Sounds stupid in that example, but is there a difference?

Not long after my special assignment ended and I returned to my position at the Washington Federal office, I received a call to report to Gordon Moodie's office. When I arrived and was escorted into his office, there were several other officials present. Gordon spent a few minutes lauding the job I had done and thanked me for the personal sacrifices I had made while being away from my family. Concluding, he stated that I had done the corporation a great service and for that I was being awarded an "outstanding contribution" award.

When the meeting ended, he asked me to stay so that he could take me to lunch. At lunch, he said that corporate wanted me to head up their equal opportunity program. He said he turned them down because he wanted me to become IBM's first black branch manager. I replied that, given the opportunity, I would rather become a branch manager. I also stated that there are many blacks that I felt were more highly qualified in the equal opportunity field, whereas my background was in sales. He asked me to return to Washington and he would see that I would be given a branch.   Returning to Washington, the new manager of the Washington Federal office called a meeting of the entire office. He echoed Gordon Moodie's words, telling everyone what I had accomplished over the last few months for the corporation. He then announced that I had also received a substantial cash award for my achievements

Now anyone would think that after receiving so many plaudits, along with the assurance from the division president that I would become the corporation's first black branch manager, that the road towards my promotion should be smooth and fast. True for others but not for me. As T.G. had forwarned, "The more you accomplish, the greater threat you will be. And those who cannot accept a black person in a position of authority, will do everything they can to stop you or any other black".

It took almost ten months before I was promoted to "branch manager", and it was ten months warding off obstacles and devious actions to prevent my promotion. Since joining IBM, I knew there would be many confrontations because of my race, and despite T.G.'s warnings, I never fully realized at that time, the determination of many in upper management that a black was not ready to manage whites and the schemes that were planned to keep it from happening.

After my luncheon meeting with Gordon Moodie, I was called to the office of the Vice President of Sales. Here was a dynamic individual, smart and aggressive, blunt and outspoken. From what I eventually learned in dealing with him, he was superb in practically every area of business except in his judgements of character. In my opinion, this is where he failed. Initially, he seemed so open with me, that my tendency was to trust him. This I did, until, as time passed and impediments began to appear, I sensed that the shots being fired at me were coming from the side I was with, and he was it's commander. I respected his expertise as a sales executive, but eventualy recognized that his actions condoned the harrassment I endured for years to come.

After exchanging a few pleasantries, he started leafing through a computer run-off of all the branch offices. He would pinpoint a certain branch and then explain why he couldn't replace that manager. This went on for about twenty minutes, until he finally folded up the sheets, explaining he needed more time to determine what branch I would be assigned. Before leaving, he promised to work on it as soon as possible. In the meantime, I should return to Washington and pick up where I left off. Years later I learned that my former Disrict Manager in Chicago, Jack Blaisdell, was trying to get approval for me to manage the Hammond, Indiana office in his district during the same period. Of course, it wasn't approved.

Soon after my special assignment, my program manager, Mike Langan, was promoted. In my opinion and going from his record, Mike became a highly competent branch manager in Norfolk, not only setting sales records but developing many future managers in the business. The new manager of the Federal Office appointed a new manager of the program where I was assigned. Since returning to Washington, my new manager never visited an account with me, never reviewed or discussed my activities in the field or, in plain words, didn't know what business activity I had going or what I had planned. He was friendly when we met, but I had no idea what he was thinking. Some time later, however, in a blind letter, I did receive a copy of an evaluation (that I wasn't aware of} where he stated that I wasn't capable of managing people. How many people in the upper echelons received a copy, I don't know. But I would guess it received wide distribution. The mistake made was that they also sent it to an "unknown" friend, who mailed me a copy. (I was never notified of this evaluation).It didn't take long for the campaign to "strip me of my recently won medals" and prove that a black was not ready to manage a branch office.

While waiting to hear from the Vice President of sales, I was sent to our sales school in New York City as a guest instructor for three weeks. Sales school had made a great improvement since my class in 1952, and I enjoyed this assignment. Management in Sales School told me I did a great job and I received many compliments from the students. However, I received no compliments or word from my management. This did not help their case against me so was

51

ignored. I decided to remain positive and patient. I had nothing to prove my case so I would wait for my adversary's to stumble, and I didn't have to wait long.

Very few changes are usually made in branch office management late in the year. Offices are attempting to reach their quota's so top management tries not to disrupt their activities. For this reason, I remained hopeful even though it was nearing the end of 1963 and I received no word from the Vice President of Sales. Nearing the end of the lst quarter of 1964, I still received no word and began to feel a little apprehensive. Everyone was leaving town to attend IBM's 100% Club, so I decided to wait until it was concluded.

Soon after, I went in to see the Washington Federal manager, who I assumed knew of the committment made to me by Gordon Moodie. I didn't mention Gordon Moodies name. Instead I said I was concerned that I hadn't heard from the Vice President of Sales. . After a few days, the Washington Federal manager called me into his office, greeted me with a big smile and announced: "Good news Lionel, we promoted your program manager to New England and we're offering you his position as program manager. (They stumbled) The Program Manager promoted was the one who wrote the "blind" evaluation stating my inability to manage. Despite this evaluation, their now offering me a position to manage. A position, that if I accepted, would mean that my promotion to branch manager could be delayed one to two years. It would also mean I could further be judged, (as my program manager judged me), by personal observation rather than, as a branch manager, by quota performance, by the same group that concocted the "blind" evaluation. Once again, as management frequently did during my entire career, they misjudged my tenacity. I said thank you but no thank you, walked out of the office, and called the president of our division, Gordon Moodie. Now I had a reason to call the Division President.

During our luncheon, nine months ago, he had given me permission   to call him directly whenever I felt it was necessary.(This was the first of many critical calls to Gordon). When I explained to Gordon what had happened since our

52

luncheon, he apologized and said that he had dropped the ball and should have followed up, personally, to see that I was assigned a branch office. Within a couple of days, I received a call from the Vice President of Sales notifying me that I was being promoted as branch manager of the Camden, New Jersey office.

A time for celebration? That is what I thought. With most promotions there are always some who disagree. I was ready to deal with that. With my promotion I felt certain that my antagonists would withdraw and let me do my job. I was to soon learn that my present exhilarant state of mind caused me to be somewhat naive, for my immediate bosses apparently had regrouped and set new plans for my failure. The warning did come from my friend and mentor, T.G.

CHAPTER VI

"PROGRAMMED FOR FAILURE"

Knowing that my friend and mentor, T. G. Laster, would not speak freely over a company phone, I waited until that evening to call at his home. T. G. gave me some sage advise and forewarned me that being in a position as the first Negro to manage a branch office, I should remember that there will be some who will do everything they can to make you fail, simply because they believe no Negro should be in a position to manage white people. He continued: "If they succeed in contributing to your failure, and you succumb quietly, their goal would have been accomplished, proving that "we can't compete in the major leagues". "Once your beaten and subdued, your then in the position where they want you. You won't be fired. You'll be given another position so they'll have you around to confirm that they were right. For those who will oppose your promotion, they will be making two big mistakes. One, they have underestimated your abilities and desire to succeed and secondly, knowing you as I do, you will not surrender your pride and sacrifice this opportunity to open the door for others that will follow you. As for those whose actions indicate unfriendliness, cooperate, so no one can accuse you of having the wrong attitude. Be fair, do your job and follow company policy. Some obstacles that your detractors place in your way, if you can hurdle them without a protest, do it. When those obstacles don't work, bigger ones will come, forcing you to protest to higher management. If you're right, higher management will agree with you. You will have won and lost. By winning, you will gain a title, none of which will be complimentary. This will follow you through your career. Everything you do will be closely scrutinized. searching for a mistake, so those who you challenged can nail you to a cross. What you would have won is what you already have, your pride. I wish you the best and stay in touch".

In a nutshell, T. G. added to what John Borican had once told me: "If you have to jump 6 ft. to qualify, you better jump 6 1/2 feet". What T.G. was adding is that if they raise the bar to unreachable heights and you protest, those referee's will engrave your name on their s--t list and will use every opportunity to find fault with your performance. So, here I go, into the arena with the lions. At the time, feeling a "high" from at last getting a branch, I listened to T.G., but felt a little more positive about the support I would receive from my superiors. As I was to later learn, T.G. was not only right in his warnings, they could have been stronger.

The branch manager I was replacing, (also a member of my 1952 sales class) was being promoted to Assistant branch manager of the St. Louis office. The St. Louis office, in comparison to Camden, was a much larger branch that required an assistant branch manager. (Later, while he was cleaning out his desk and discussing the personnel with me, he kept repeating: "you know, Lionel, they keep telling me this is a promotion, but I'm going from branch manager to assistant branch manager. I can't figure it out." I wasn't about to explain to him that he was caught in a "panic" situation where some move had to be made.

I arrived at the Philadelphia Airport on a Thursday afternoon in early June. I was met by the district manager and new boss, and his assistant. My flight was running late and he let me know, jokingly, that if it was much later, they would have had to carry him out of the lounge. I wasn't too certain as to what he meant until we got in the car. He appeared high on liquor and I was high thinking about my new challenge.

IBM was always very secretive about promotion announcements. No one in the Camden office knew I was coming. All they knew was that they had to be at an 8:30 meeting. To maintain the secrecy, the District Manager took me to his home in the suburbs of Philadephia, to stay overnight. By the time we arrived, his wife, who I found to be very gracious, had dinner waiting. By then he said he needed another drink to relax. Not asking what I wanted, he poured a water glass, three quarters full of scotch, for both of us. Before I knew it, he was on his second glass. In the meantime, I said I couldn't drink scotch "straight", so meandered over to the sink and making sure I wasn't noticed, poured most of it down the sink and filled the glass with water. We had to rise early in order to get to Camden by 8:00 a.m., so after I was shown my room, he practically staggered to bed. Arising early the next morning, I went to close the window since it had gotten a little cold. Suddenly I heard this big splash, and there was my new boss, splashing in a pool that must have been as, a friend often said, "as cold as a witches tail".. When I came downstairs, I was surprised to see that he looked as if he never took a drink in his life. He was bright, alert and had completely recovered from drinking enough that would floor most people for days.

The announcement meeting went off well. The office was located in downtown Camden adjacent to the main, and probably the oldest, hotel in Camden.. The location could have been a furniture store in the past. Camden, itself, was deteriorating. Families who could afford it were fleeing to the suburbs, leaving the city to the poor. The two largest industries were Campbell Soups and the RCA Corporation. I soon was able to learn, by the scent in the air, the kind of soup Campbell was canning that day.

The Camden office covered the lower third of New Jersey. West, from the Delaware river to east, the Atlantic shoreline.

I was shocked to see what I was assigned. As the Manager I was replacing outlined it, there were six sales representatives, two were fairly new and needed training, with one of the new salesmen having severe back problems and frequently out sick. One senior salesman had severe stomach problems and was on sick leave, leaving only three salesmen who, at the time, were capable of carrying a quota.

I also discovered that with my announcement they had cut my administrative staff. The cut was so deep that my secretary had to also take over the required needs of the sales staff. Lori Truitt was one of the most efficient administrative persons I've worked with. After a year, she resigned because she was overworked. Not long after I arrived in Camden, and we got to know each other, she asked if she could see me for a few minutes.

57

As Lori explained the events: "The administration manager called me into his office before your announcement. Your boss, the District Manager was also present. They explained to me that a Negro was being installed as branch manager, and they would understand if I objected to working with one. And if I did, they would see that I was placed in a similar position. Mr. Fultz, I was very offended. On their own, their statements assumed that I was prejudiced. I made it clear to them that I would be happy to work with you." During our conversation she let it be known that they were both shocked.

So here I am, the first black branch manager in IBM, starting off with a crippled sales force and a depleted administrative staff. I did get a call from the Vice President of Sales soon after my installation. He wished me luck and I in turn asked what advice does he give a new branch manager. He replied: "No matter what you observe, try not to make any decisions for at least thirty days". As it happened, this turned out to be excellent advice.

The senior salesman in Camden was an individual I learned to respect a great deal. As mentioned previously, despite the saying that you had to be part of the "Irish Mafia" to move in our division, Jack McDermott's heritage didn't help him. Jack was an excellent salesman who had all the attributes you look for. He was intelligent, stable and hard-working, highly respected by his co-workers, a very agreeable person amd always willing to assist and help out. Soon after arriving in Camden, I happened to notice that whenever I entered the office, Jack would disappear. But he was always there when I arrived. In my mind, I began to worry about the amount of time he spent in the office. As a salesman quickly learns, the customers aren't inside our office, but outside. Depite my temptation to sit down and talk with Jack, I remembered the Sales Managers advice; "Wait 30 days." I decided to wait 60 days, because I had many other problems to face and gaining the confidence of my co-workers was a high priority.

Around six weeks after arriving, I was having lunch with another of the senior representatives who I really learned to respect. I could sense that he was beginning to respect me. We were having lunch in between calls when I asked "I'm having a problem that perhaps you may be able to help me with. And perhaps you can also help a friend. If you agree, I would like it to be strictly confidential". He agreed. I continued; "My problem is that I can't understand why Jack McDermott seems tied to the office. He's a very proud person and I don't want to do or say anything that would hurt rather than help. Do you have an answer?"

I was told a very interesting story of how, for several years, Jack had been doing much of the branch managers work. He was even calling on some accounts that were the managers responsibility. In short, until I arrrived, Jack was playing the role of branch manager and was habitually in the office. With my arrival, Jack's work habits were immediately thrown into a turmoil. Clearly, he was having difficulty returning to his activities as a salesman. With better insight, I was able to take a much different approach in discussing the situation with Jack.

When we met, I told him that I was aware of the great help he was to my predecessor in handling many of his responsibilities. I continued: "I realize you did this on a voluntary basis, Jack, but being a commission salesman, didn't it have some impact on your earnings? The reason I mention this is that, considering your experience, I would like to call on your assistance when needed, but not in a way that it impacts your earnings." He replied: "Lionel, I appreciate your thoughts. I've had a problem adjusting. Being given additional responsibilities is helpful for one's ego, but I still have to make a living. I will be available to assist you, but my first priority will be "selling something". The Vice President of Sales gave me good advice to "wait thirty day's". It benefitted me, but more important, in the long run it benefitted the salesman.

The first few months in Camden were very difficult, business wise. Initially, I spent a great deal of time meeting with the salesmen, one on one. So we could get to know each other, but also to get a feel for their needs. With one on sick-leave, one unable to work full-time and a third, new in the territory and needing a lot of help, my task wasn't going to be easy. To make matters worse, the cut that was made in my administrative staff

59

made it difficult to provide the necessary back-up for the salesmen. Though our group operated independently, the "landlord" manager for Camden was the data-processing branch manager. This gave him control of administration, with the administration manager reporting to him. Since my boss, the District Manager, , had cut my administration "head-count", the administration manager supported his action and offered me no support. This, despite the fact that my secretary, Lori Truitt, who was always evaluated "outstanding", constantly complained of being overworked since the cut took place. Despite my complaints regarding administrative support, no help was given.

Our office was far behind on quota when I took over. Camden, like many cities in the northeast during the sixties, was going through detrimental changes that affected the salesmen covering the city. Businesses were moving out enmass. Some moved into areas still within our branch's territory, but many moved completely out of our office's territory, with no business replacements moving in. When the two salesmen handling the city of Camden made me aware of this, I immediately expanded their territory to cushion their losses. Both were excellent salesmen, but needed time to properly impact their new areas. Since they knew I was aware of this, they were concerned about their quota position but knew I understood the situation. Once again, as T.G. predicted, an assault was about to take place. The multiple problems I had inherited, if given time and support from my superiors, I felt could be overcome. I received neither the time or the support, only a cut in my administrative support staff. When taking over the branch, I was advised by a good friend in management that if any issue was used to "shoot me down" it would be employee's morale". He was right. What my superiors didn't realize that since my arrival I had worked hard to gain the confidence of those I worked with. The powder that they thought was "explosive" was really wet. It was a major confrontation. One that eventually ended in the division Presidents office. One that I won but, in a sense, I lost. I may have been on the S list before, but after this confrontation, my name was probably engraved on it, right in the center of a big target.

I had been manager of the Camden office for approximately seven months, when I received a call from the District Manager's secretary that he would like to conduct an executive interview with two of the salesmen, the ones who were working the City of Camden area and were behind quota. I notified the salesmen that they were to meet, individually, with my boss, the district manager, the next morning. Naturally they were a little nervous, considering their quota position, so I reassured them that these interviews are required and its purpose is mainly to hear what's on the mind of the one being interviewed.

The two interviews were conducted in a private office, and lasted approximately one hour. As soon as the interviews were over, my District Manager called me into the office to give me an unexpected formal evaluation. All employee's receive an evaluation once a year by their manager. The evaluation is based on a performance plan they are given at the beginning of the evaluation year. The ratings are Outstanding, Exceeds requirements, Meets Requirements and Unsatisfactory. When you're placed on unsatisfactory, you're usually given a plan that you have to meet during the next 30 to 60 days. Your superior should also relate to you, specifically and with supporting data, why he believes your performance is unsatisfactory. You should also be given the opportunity to discuss and, if deemed unwarranted, challenge the evaluation. During my career as a manager, I evaluated no less than ten as unsatisfactory. In each case I worked with the individual in the field before the evaluation, making recommendations as to how they could improve their performance. *I would also ask them to put in writing,"what management can do to help improve their performance". What assistance they needed to improve their skills, they would get. If everything failed, I would then evaluate their performance "unsatisfactory". Even then, I would make every effort to assist them during the 30 to 60 day period. Of those I deemed unsatisfactory, five were released from the business. On one release, I was overruled by my district manager, and they transferred him to another office. (I was to later learn that he caused IBM all kinds of legal problems (that had nothing to do with me) at his new location before he finally left the business). Four improved their performance, one becoming a manager and another became a division director.*

I walked into the office that my District Manager was using and was hardly seated, when he spoke:"Lionel, I just interviewed two of your salesmen and they complained that you haven't been giving them the support they needed. They can't get their typing done and the morale of the office is low. Here's your evaluation which I just completed. I consider your performance "unsatisfactory". You can read and sign it, and return it to my office". He snatched his briefcase up and walked out.

I now know how it feels to be "bushwacked".I was stunned but not unconscious. If he thought I was down for the ten count without fighting back, he was mistaken. I asked Lori to hold my calls while I read the performance plan. It was obvious to me that it was written before he visited the office. I wasn't certain as to how I would defend myself against what I considered the initial attack to prove that a "Negro" couldn't manage an IBM branch office. Though prejudice was rampant in our society in 1964, I didn't want to use that as my defense because that is what is always expected. What most of those who are prejudiced don't often expect is a defense based on facts. Before I knew it, (I had been sitting there contemplating my strategy for over an hour) someone knocked on the door

It was almost twelve o'clock and it was one of the salesmen who the District Manager had interviewed. He asked me if we could go next door to the hotel and have lunch. I could see he was very upset so I agreed. All I could do was to sit and wait for him to start talking, which he did as soon as the waitress left after bringing our order. "Lionel, I had to talk to you, but didn't want to come back to the office until your boss left. I was a nervous wreck last night. I couldn't sleep. Because of my quota position, I thought he was coming over to fire me. In fact, I was flabbergasted when I realized that it was you he was after, and I must confess, somewhat relieved. He opened up the interview by strongly criticizing you and then looking for my concurrence. He made nothing but leading statements. "I understand the morale is very low"...Lionel comes in late every day" ..."doesen't listen to your problems"...etc., I was afraid to disagree with him because of the intensity of his accusations. You've been very fair with me ever since your arrival. I feel everyone thinks the same. I think you were screwed in getting this office, considering the personnel situation. You have some good people working for you. All they need is some strong support". Later, the same day, the other salesman who was interviewed, came to see me with practically the same story. (These two salesmen became my strongest supporters, with one going into management.)

I started to pick up the phone and make my move, but instead decided to sleep on it, and wait until the next day. The next morning I called the Vice President of Sales and asked to see him. He knew I wouldn't call unless it was a critical situation. He probably surmised that my District Manager was involved since I didn't bring my problem to him. In a second, he said he would be in Philadelphia the next day, and to look for his call.

I waited most of the day for his call and I was beginning to think that he had changed his plans. The call finally came around 4:30 PM and he gave me the room number at the Marriott Hotel on City Line Avenue in Philadelphia. I didn't get there until nearly 6:00, due to the rush hour traffic. When I entered the room, my District Manager was also there. When he last left my office, he didn't even say "goodbye". Now he greeted me with a big smile as if he was seeing a long lost friend.

The Vice President of Sales got right down to business. Since I asked for the meeting, he told me to speak first. I did, realizing that my boss probably spent most of the afternoon building his case without my being able to defend myself. I didn't know that for certain so I avoided mentioning it. As I spoke, the Vice President acted as if he was totally unaware of the conditions I walked into in Camden. He seemed shocked when I mentioned what support I had gotten from the district, which was zero. He also didn't know that my boss had cut my administrative staff 50%, causing a serious problem in getting our paperwork out. The more I talked, the more the District Managers smile disappeared, to the point where he was frowning. Suddenly, without warning, in the middle of a subject I was covering, my

63

boss blurted out: "my wife's got steaks on the grill and we better get out of here while they're hot". At that. I stopped talking, reached for my hat and coat and apologized to the Vice President for keeping him from his dinner. He was enraged and turned to my boss and shouted: "Will you shut the hell up and sit down". He then turned to me, apologized and told me to continue and take my time. I replied: "Are you sure, I don't want to keep you both from your dinner?" He assured me it was okay but one could easily sense his displeasure towards my boss for "letting the cat out of the bag".

As I could see then and was later affirmed by future events, the Vice President of Sales and my boss were very close friends. My last question to him was if he ever heard of a one minute evaluation? When he answered no, I told him he just heard of one. He was so peeved that he reached for the evaluation, ripped it up and told me to forget it and just go back and run the Camden office. He also asked me to call him direct if I had any further problems. It was around 6:45PM when I left, so I guess they had to eat cold steaks.

For the next year, business steadily picked up in the Camden office. In a district of 23 branch offices that included New Jersey, Pennsylvania, Delaware, Maryland, District of Columbia, Virginia and North Carolina, Camden was usually at the bottom of the totem pole. We had a long ways to go, but I felt I had the right people who could eventually accomplish our goals. The biggest obstacle to accomplishing our goals was coming to be my boss, the District Manager.

There are many things you can't do without the district managers approval. After the meeting with the Vice President, my boss stopped communicating with me, altogether. At managers meetings, he acted as if I wasn't there. Even if I met him in an elevator, he wouldn't speak. I would leave messages with his secretary, and he wouldn't return my call. One time I had a critical personnel situation that only he could rule on, and he wouldn't return my call. I called his secretary everyday for almost a week, with no reply, She kept making excuses for him and promised me he would call. Finally, around 2:00AM in the morning, my phone rang..I couldn't understand what the caller was saying, because, from the sound of his voice, I gathered that he was in a drunken stupor. I finally recognized the District Managers voice. I still couldn't make out what he was saying, but for the first time, despite our altercations, I pitied him because he obviouisly had a serious drinking problem and was ill. This was happening during a very critical period in my personal life.

My father had a serious stroke that left him partially paralyzed during the time when I was first settling in the Camden office. From time to time, I would drive up to Newark, New Jersey on week-ends to check on his condition. Arriving home from one of these visits, I found my wife having terrible pains and unable to move. I put in an emergency call for an ambulance and called our family physician. The initial diagnosis at the hospital was pleurisy, but luckily our family physician thought differently. Treating her for pleurlisy might have been fatal. By the next morning there were signs that indicated that she had thrombo phlebitis, with blood clots in her lungs. For the next three years she had to have several serious operations. During this time I had to hire housekeepers to help me with my two daughters, who were both in grammar school. My daily schedule was rising early enough to get my daughters ready for school. Leaving for the office. Shopping on my way home from the office. Relieving the housekeeper. Cooking dinner. Getting a babysitter.. Going to the hospital to visit my wife. Getting back home around 10PM. Looking back I wondered how I managed to take care of my family's needs and still work and devise plans to develop business in the branch.

My boss's drinking problems was no big secret to his superiors so it seemed futile to complain. He was sick and it seemed senseless leaving him in such a position of responsibility. I could do nothing, since I soon learned that proving someone is an alcoholic is difficult if they deny it. IBM would not put anyone into a program for alcoholism unless the individual admitted it was a problem. Until they eventually transferred him to a lower level job, I frequently saw him at conferences, so inebriated, that he couldn't balance himself. At an exhibit in Philadelphia, while with a higher executive, I saw him slip and almost fall

65

down some stairs. I'm sorry to say that whoever thought they were protecting him, were actually causing more harm by not persuading him to enter a treatment program.

As expected, my boss was eventually demoted and transferred to Washington, D. C. as a branch manager. The word was that he had asked for the transfer. I can't understand the reasoning for transferring someone with a problem to another position where his disabilities would be more apparent since he would be dealing directly with salesmen. Unhappily, this transfer affected me, indirectly. More important, it affected someone that I greatly respected.

One of the salesmen in Camden developed to the point where I strongly recommended him for a management position. If my recommendation was approved, I would have no control as to where he's assigned. He was assigned to Washington, as a marketing manager, reporting to my old boss. Sometime later, I met him at an IBM meeting and he informed me that he might have to go back to sales. He said his choice was his position or his family. He explained that practically every night his boss insisted that he go for a drink with him. From being a good family man, he found himself arriving home late, and not in the condition that pleased his wife. He went back to sales and IBM lost an individual that I thought had great potential. A loss that should never have happened.

By the year 1967, IBM had greatly increased the number of new black employee's, especially in my division, Office Products. The president of our division and the one responsible for my promotion, Gordon Moodie, wasn't just talking about what should be done in hiring blacks, but was putting pressure on his Vice Presidents to make certain the corporations directives were followed. The best move that Gordon Moodie made was to name Earl Wilson, a very successful IBM salesman in St. Louis, as the divisions first equal opportunity manager. With Gordon's backing, Earl pushed our division to the forefront in recruiting many "high potential" black employee's. By 1967 through aggressive recruiting, IBM was leading the way within Corporate America.

Without having to constantly look over my shoulder, by 1967 I had recruited some excellent sales representatives, doubled the staff and with the great teamwork of customer engineering, administration and sales, we had left the back of the pack and were swiftly heading towards the front runners. Little did I realize or expect that my success would cause renewed concerns with my bosses.

United States
of America

Vol. 130   WASHINGTON, MONDAY, JANUARY 23, 1984   No. 1

Congressional Record

TRIBUTE TO LIONEL FULTZ

HON. WILLIAM (BILL) CLAY
OF MISSOURI
IN THE HOUSE OF REPRESENTATIVES
Monday, January 23, 1984

Mr. CLAY. Mr. Speaker, Mr. Lionel Fultz just recently announced his retirement form IBM Corp. after 34 years. Mr. Fultz was one of the first black salesmen hired by IBM. He started his career in Chicago, Ill., in 1950. His achievements in IBM were numerous. He qualified for IBM's highest market achievements which were: 5 Golden Circles, 14 One Hundred Percent Clubs, and was named Branch Manager of the Year in 1968-69.

Lionel Fultz is a very unique individual because he was always involved in helping young blacks get into the corporate world. He received the company's Outstanding Contribution Award for his efforts in assisting the company's efforts in recruiting black employees.

Lionel has received numerous citations for his community endeavors. He is a former board member of the Morgan State University Foundation, board member of National Conference of Christians and Jews, Employment Practices Commission of Washington Board of Trade, Montessori Schools of Maryland, and Minority Business Council of Baltimore.

Lionel is past president of the United Negro College Fund, State of Maryland; director and vice chairman, National Alliance of Business, D.C. Metro 1976-77; vice president, Washington Urban League 1978; past president, Toastmasters International, Chicago; division director, United Way of Baltimore.

He is presently a board member and member of executive committee, Keswick Home for Incurables, Columbia, Md., board member of Voluntary Council for Equal Opportunity, and president of NEW START—a nonprofit voluntary organization dedicated to the education and rehabilitation of prison inmates.

Lionel lives in Columbia, Md., with his wife Betty, and two daughters, Kathy and Marlene.

I am inserting this article so that it may be available to young men and women across this country and serve as guidance and inspiration as they seek to achieve their life's goals.

William S. Callion, Jr.
26200 Lahser Road, Southfield, Michigan 48076

April 28, 1977

Dear Lionel,

Words cannot express the happiness that I feel in
your recent opportunity as Executive Director of the
Washington Metropolitan National Alliance for Business.
I am certain that my sentiments are echoed by hundreds
of people who know the contributions you have made to
the IBM Corporation and the inspiration you've been to
other people who are unwilling to compromise and very
willing to speak the truth.

I am very certain that you will make an equally significant contribution for yourself and for the IBM
Corporation and the community in your new assignment.

When you help yourself, you help all of us.

Sincerely,

Bill

Mr. Lionel Fultz
IBM Corporation
100 E. Pratt Street
Baltimore, Maryland 21202

69

Frank T. Cary

Old Orchard Road, Armonk, New York 10504

September 1, 1980

Dear Lionel,

Congratulations on your thirtieth service anniversary with IBM!

This is a significant anniversary in your career, and I want to express my personal appreciation for the many contributions you have made to IBM. The achievements of fourteen Hundred Percent Clubs and a Golden Circle, coupled with your 1963 Outstanding Contribution Award and 1969 Manager of the Year Award, are career highlights of which you can be justifiably proud. These accomplishments within IBM, as well as your service to the National Alliance of Businessmen and the Washington Urban League, are greatly appreciated.

Thank you for your dedication and please accept my best wishes for the future.

Sincerely,

Frank Cary

Mr. L. R. Fultz
IBM Corporation
10215 Fernwood Road
Suite 206
Bethesda, MD 20034

IBM – C.E.O.

70

T. B. Barton

225 West Virginia Beach Boulevard. Norfolk. Virginia 23510

May 2, 1977

Dear Lionel,

Congratulations on the recent announcement of being named the Executive Director of the National Alliance of Businessmen.

I know it must be most gratifying to see your efforts and contributions to IBM recognized in this manner.

As one of the many whose careers you have given impetus, I would again like to express my appreciation.

Please accept my best wishes for continued success.

Sincerely,

Mr. Lionel R. Fultz

F. E. Jackson, Jr.
P. O. Box 6673, Orange, California 92667

February 14, 1975

Dear Lionel,

It was with the greatest pleasure that I heard a testimonial function was to be held in your honor. I really wanted to be there and tried several different ways to make it.

When I knew I wouldn't be able to attend in person, I said I would send a telegram to arrive, hopefully, at just the right moment. However, would you believe what happened to me that day? I had forgotten my own wedding anniversary! You can imagine the rest.

Since then, I have heard the affair was simply outstanding and I couldn't be happier about that. Please let me convey my congratulations for the recognition you received and so richly deserve, as well as my own personal thanks for the many times you and I haved talked. I always came away from those sessions with the feeling I had been helped just a little bit further in my ambitions and aspirations.

There is no question in my mind that you not only deserve the accolades you received but much more. I will never forget you, and my intent is to never let you forget that I appreciate the things you've done for all of us.

Sincerely,

Mr. L. R. Fultz
OP Branch Manager
IBM Corporation
One Investment Place
Towson, MD 21204

JUN 23 1978

Mr. Lionel Fultz
Metro Director,
National Alliance of Businessmen
1129 20th Street, N.W.
Washington, D.C. 20036

Dear Mr. Fultz:

The D.C. Department of Manpower would like to give public
recognition to you for your outstanding contribution to
its efforts in the manpower field at a ceremony Wednesday,
June 28, 1978, Main Labor Department Auditorium, 200
Constitution Avenue, N.W., at 1:00 p.m.

The Honorable Walter E. Washington will be the distinguished
speaker for this occasion.

On behalf of the Department of Manpower, I am inviting you
to attend this ceremony to accept your recognition and
socialize with us.

Sincerely yours,

THOMAS A. WILKINS
Director

73

Fultz Marketing Consultants, Inc.
10955 Swansfield Road
Columbia, Maryland 21044
301-596-3957

June 29, 1988.

Dear Earl:

It's amazing how difficult it is to write a letter of congratulations when there is so much to say. You just don't know where to begin. However, Earl, I'll start by thanking you for the thousands in IBM who have benefited due to the pioneering and aggressive programs you insisted IBM adopt if they were to have a meaningful equal opportunity program. Unfortunately, there were some who disagreed with your recommendations to accelerate the promotion of key talented blacks, ie., Al Martin, Bill Goins, Cynthia Adams, whom we lost to Xerox and are now V.P.'s, among many others. So once again, let me speak for all those, from coast to coast, within and outside of IBM, who have reaped the fruits of your efforts and your sacrifices, you were the best and you always gave your best and no words can express our appreciation.

In Denver,Colorado, around 1960, Tom Watson Jr., made his famous "wild duck" speech in which he pleaded for some of us to become "wild ducks", to disagree when you thought the company was going the wrong way, regardless of the consequences, (even if it meant that you might get shot down). His reasoning; "if IBM was to survive, we've got to know our weaknesses, our obstacles and our errors". I was the only black in the audience, but your spirit must have been there, Earl, because you have been the exact mold of what Tom Watson was looking for. And as he prophesized, the "wild ducks", over the years, did bring tremendous benefits to the company, and as he also prophesized, most were shot down.

But you've been literally wounded, tarred and feathered, ambushed and raped, but still survived. From one wounded "wild duck" to another, it's been twenty-five years, and still the "real" recognition you truly deserve has not appeared. Hopefully, in the near future, IBM will express appreciation for your many contributions and sacrifices to make IBM a greater company.

To a geat and most valuable friend, congratulations on your 25th anniversary with IBM, (and don't fly too low).

Sincerely

l i o n e l

Lionel R. Fultz
10955 Swansfield Road
Columbia, Md. 21044

To: Earl Wilson

74

western union **Mailgram**

MICHAEL E KALOGRIS
8609 ALVERSTONE WAY
AUSTIN TX 78759

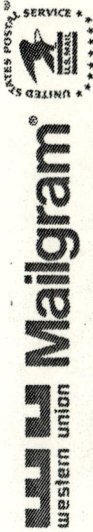

2-0369161131 05/11/77 ICS IPMBNGZ CSP BALB
5123452378 MGM TDBN AUSTIN TX 100 05-11 0250P EST

MR LIONEL FULTZ CARE OF BOB BRADY
100 EAST PRATT ST
BALTIMORE MD 21202

LIZ AND I WOULD LIKE TO EXTEND OUR WARMEST CONGRATULATIONS FOR YOUR NEW
ASSIGNMENT. I WILL ALWAYS BE GRATEFUL TO YOU FOR TEACHING ME THE
FUNDAMENTALS FOR BECOMING A GOOD BUSINESSMAN. BEST WISHES FOR YOUR
CONTINUED SUCCESS.

SINCERELY YOURS,

MIKE KALOGRIS

14:50 EST

MGMCOMP MGM

75

≡≡≡ Mailgram®

western union

MAILGRAM SERVICE CENTER
MIDDLETOWN, VA. 22645

1-024061M131 05/11/77 ICS IPMDVKA DVR BALA
01093 MGM DENVER CO 100 05-11 127P MDT

BOB BRADY
IBM 100 E PRATT ST
BALTIMORE MD 21202

DEAR BOB:
    PLEASE PASS ON MY CONGRATULATIONS TO LIONEL ABOUT
HIS NEW ASSIGNMENT.
    IT WAS MY PLEASURE TO FULFILL A CHALLENGING JOB FOR
A BRANCH MANAGER THAT MADE HARD WORK FUN
    BEST OF LUCK LIONEL
REGARDS
    MURRAY RUFFELL
14:52 EST

MGMCOMP MGM

76

IBM

International Business Machines Corporation

4601 Park Road
Charlotte, North Carolina 28209

April 28, 1977

Mr. Lionel Pultz
Branch Manager
Office Products Division
IBM Corporation
100 East Pratt Street
Baltimore, MD

Dear Lionel:

Congratulations on your recent appointment to the National Alliance of
Businessmen. There's no doubt that the people that will be working with
you will benefit from your business knowledge and from your open and
warm personality.

It's hard to put into words exactly what you've meant to me personally
and to my career with IBM. I only hope that you will share the personal
involvement that you gave me with whomever you work with in your new
assignment. Thank you for the wonderful memories.

Sincerely yours,

Jesse Greene
Marketing Manager
Office Products Division

JG/gr

77

Chapter VII

"Success without Medals"

Our new district manager and my former boss was quite a contrast. He didn't drink or smoke and jogged every morning. The change was such a relief that I tried my best to be friendly. His demeanor when we were together was that of a four star general looking down his nose at a 2nd lieutenant. He never seemed interested in what I had to say. It wasn't long before I would sometimes get the impression that he had pre-judged me. Being self-critical, I ignored those feelings, attributing them to the after-affects of my experiences with my last boss. I had forgotten T.G.'s warning that I could win a battle, but in so doing, gain a prominent spot on the S list of those in power.

By 1968, the Cherry Hill office not only left the bottom of the totem pole, but we were moving towards the top. Since the district kept the records of all the offices, no one knew their standing until the district manager released the figures. Our new district manager said he was coming over to conduct some executive interviews. By this time, our sales force had doubled and business was booming. I was benefitting from a great sales force.

Managing salesmen is challenging because everyone is different. With some salesmen, you don't come across unless you scream at them and bang your fist on the desk. With some, its the worst thing you can do. Being human, sometimes I erred in dealing with those I managed. The one thing I always tried to not err in was showing my respect for every individual. No matter what happened, before I pronounced my decision I would always ask the individual:"Perhaps there's something I don't understand or I'm not aware of that caused the problem?" Frequently I heard some legitimate reasons that changed my thinking.

79

Years ago, an old timer in the business who I greatly respected told me the story of a branch manager who was removed from his position for making the wrong decision when everything indicated that it was the right one. The salesman in question had a unsatisfactory rating and had to improve in the next 60 days or face dismissal from the business. He and his branch manager were to make a presentation for a large data processing system to be sold to a bank. He and the branch manager rehearsed the presentation the day before. The branch manager told him to take the charts home so he could continue rehearsing, and meet him at the bank at 9:00 because they were to present to the board of directors at 9:30. The branch manager arrived at the bank at 9:00 and the salesman wasn't there. He waited until 9;15 and then called the office. He hadn't called. By 9:30 his secretary hadn't heard from the salesman and couldn't locate him. The customer waited until 9:45, then the manager had to apologize. He returned to the office and waited until closing time for the salesman to call. The call never came. He was able to reach the salesman's wife, and she thought he was with him. The manager left a message for the salesman, if and when he came in the next day, that he was fired. The manager reacted prematurely. He made a decision without waiting to hear what happened to the salesman. The branch manager was demoted and the salesman rehired.

Just as the salesman was about to leave home to meet his manager, his family physician called and asked if he could stop by his office for a minute, that it was very important. The office was on the way to the bank, and he had plenty of time because he had planned to arrive at 8:30. Two weeks before, they had taken their young daughter for a routine check-up. What the doctor told him was that his young daughter had an incurable illness that would cause her death in a matter of weeks. The salesman was so shaken, that he went into a daze and wandered the streets all day. When he returned home that evening, he couldn't recall where he had been.

When I look back, what I'm most proud of is the loyalty and respect I received from those I had the privilege to manage. During my career, I never experienced anyone going open door against me. Most problems that arose were usually caused or initiated by my superiors. The following incident is an example of loyalty and just one of many attempts by management to prove that I wasn't qualified, by searching for reasons that would prove I wasn't responsible for any success our office attained.

To repeat, 1968 was becoming a banner year for our office, which was now called the Cherry Hill branch, having moved from Camden. Our present district manager had arrived to conduct some executive interviews.The interviews were being conducted in an office several doors from mine. To describe the scene, the salesman would enter the office for the interview. After approximately 10 to 15 minutes, he would leave,(while another salesman entered), walk down to my office and close the door behind him and rant: "What the hell is going on? That S.O.B. wanted to know why our office is having such a great year and then suggested it couldn't be you (meaning me), and that someone else must be motivating the group." This was repeated over and over again.

How did I feel? After so many battles in the past with my bosses, considering how the office was doing, I was really caught off guard. Looking back, I may have been a little naive to think that a change in bosses and the success of our office would get me off the S list. Expecting laurels, an attempt was made to undermine the reputation I had with my group. After the interviews were completed, the District Manager simply said his goodbyes to the staff and left. Nothing was said regarding the offices record.

A few weeks later, early in 1969, I received a call from the district manager, instructing me to be at his office at 4:00 PM. I arrived at 3:50 and waited. He didn't come out of his office until after 5:00. Without any apology for keeping me waiting, he asked me to grab my coat and follow him. We went to his car, which was parked outside in an open lot. He opened the trunk, reached for a package, handed it to me and said, "Congratulations, Lionel, the record of your office made you manager of the year for 1968. He also handed me a check. He shook my hand, wished me a good evening, got in his car and drove away. I was dumbfounded, dismayed and angry.

81

For years, the Camden/Cherry Hill office was at the bottom, while other offices with better records, deservedly, received the recognition. For the past three and a half years, our sales force, with the assistance of customer engineering and administration working together as a team, strove to excel and gain the recognition that other offices enjoyed in the past. What reasons could I give to my co-workers for the failure of the district manager to recognize them in person? The 100% club was to start in Miami, Florida, in ten days. Previously, I had made arrangements to visit a friend in the Bahama Islands before the club. Before leaving, I sent a letter to the district manager's boss, the regional manager, describing the "parking lot" presentation and how his actions could destroy the morale of an office that had exceeded all expectations. I then took off for the Bahama's.

My trip to the Bahama's was to visit a very good personal and family friend, Terry McNeely, who resided on Paradise Island. Terry gave up a thriving business in Manhattan to assist the great actor and his long time friend, Sidney Poitier. Being very aware of the harrassment I was experiencing and the pressures they brought on, he persuaded me to pay him a visit. After leaving Nassau and arriving in Miami the day of the convention, there was my boss, looking like a nervous wreck, waiting for me in the lobby of the hotel.

He apologized profusely, as I'm sure he was instructed. I told him that the one's he really should be apologizing to were the salesmen who "busted their ass" to achieve the best record, which in the long run also greatly improved his district record. The following day, at a district breakfast where all the qualifiers and managers from all the branches were present, I thought he would never stop singing the praises of the Cherry Hill office. The practice was good, because he had to do a repeat performance the following year. Cherry Hill had achieved a "rarity". For the second year in a row we were the leading office and thanks to the efforts of the entire team, I, again, was named manager of the year.

CHAPTER VIII

"BIG BLUE'S MISSED OPPORTUNITIES"

A friend who had lost a "golden opportunity", told me he had a gold mine in his hands and did nothing with it. Which best describes IBM's position in 1970 as far as reaping the benefits by being perhaps the first major corporation to recruit black employee's.

From being the leader of the pack in recruiting top black employee's from 1963 thru 1970, the company was gradually letting "the gold mine" slip through their hands.

By 1970, with our division breaking sales records and the Chairman of the Board stating at a 100% club meeting that the Office Products division, for every dollar invested, was the most profitable division in the corporation, the division under Gordon Moodie was flying high. It came as a shock and to the dismay of many black employee's when he took an early retirement. Bart Stevens, Vice President and General Manager was named the new division president.

By 1970, the number of blacks hired in IBM had increased substantially. Most were hired in what was then renamed the Office Products Division. From electric typewriters, the division had expanded into word processing and dictation equipment. As I predicted, IBM, being one of the earliest recruiters of black employee's, hired many who were the "cream of the crop", off many of the campuses of predominantly black colleges. By 1970, some had reached 1st level management and a very few 2nd level. The road wasn't easy for many of those who were hired. But the performance of many blacks proved that it was too late to claim that "blacks couldn't play in the big leagues".

During my career, I attended one of many IBM management schools. In 1970, while attending a management school in Long Island, New York, a lecture was given by a member of IBM's

Management Committee. The management committee consisted of the three highest officials in the corporation. During the lecture, which was open to questions, he was asked if IBM would eventually move blacks into executive positions. His answer was that there would be a black vice president in IBM in a year. Fifteen years later, his prediction still hadn't come true. Some black's in IBM did become Vice Presidents, but not with IBM. We lost some extremely talented people who left in frustration when they realized thre was a glass ceiling that halted their progress once they reached a certain level.

During my special assignment when IBM initiated their program to recruit black employees, I warned our executives in writing and verbally, that you can't hire people who have the abilities to become "high potential", and then limit their opportunity to advance. I also warned that discrimination would continue to flourish in IBM if there is no penalty imposed whenever it occurs. IBM has always been a company that expected results from its managers and that includes following directives from top management.

It had now been seven years since my meeting with the Corporate Vice Presidents in White Plains. I've yet to hear of a manager being demoted or penalized for discriminatory practices. If the company treated managers who failed to meet their business objectives in the same manner, the company would have failed years ago. I was assured and the black recruits were assured, when hired, that they would have an "equal opportunity". I was deceived and so were they. IBM, being a leading international company dealing with people of every race and nationallity, really could have set a precedent if they had followed through with what they promised and stated.

If I was pictured as combatant during those years, perhaps it was true. "As they would say in the infantry, once the battle starts, its your ass or theirs." I did have some friends in headquarters. A few in higher management who got to know me but for good reason, couldn't reveal our friendship. Not long after I had made "manager of the year" for the second time in a row, one of my friends informed me that at a staff meeting I was suggested to fill an important marketing position at headquarters.

Immediately, one attendee jumped up and started tearing me apart. He even suggested (apparently not knowing of my recent successes) that I had failed as a branch manager and was having nothing but problems in Cherry Hill. My friend, who, by the way is white, apologized for not being able to defend me. He once told me, "your name is probably on more "enemy lists" than there are seeds in a watermelon.

Despite the progress, there were still managers out there who refused to change. At a 100% club, a black salesman from an office in the western region introduced himself. This was his first club and he made it a point to track me down to relate the following: "I guess my branch manager considered my making the club a fluke because he's still trying to prove that black's don't belong in the business. You know what he did? He hired this black guy off the street who was so crude you would cross the street rather than walk by him. I'd be surprised if he finished elementary school. I tried to stay away from the office whenever he was there. The story told me was that he was hired with the understanding that he must pass the tests after receiving training in the office. I understand the training was a joke. Everything was over his head. They said that what happened after the training caused an uproar. The branch manager called him into his office and should have closed the door. When he told him that he failed the tests and had to be released, he started screaming the worst profanities you can imagine, threatening the manager and screaming that he was going to get him and his family. The manager disappeared for some time and the word was that IBM arranged to move his family out of the area until things calmed down." I thought the story may have been exaggerated until I heard the same thing from other sources.

IBM's evaluation system was used to determine raises, promotions, demotions and firings. Your performance should determine your rating but this wasn't true in many cases. If a manager didn't particularly care for someone who performed well and was respected by his colleagues, he could rate him 'meets requirments' or even "exceeds requirements" and then note in his summary "not management material"..I've known outstanding blacks with high potential who left the business due to a managers personal prejudices. One, in particular, felt stopped in his tracks, resigned and went on to become a division president with one of our biggest competitors.

Early in 1970, I was called in for an evaluation by my third district manager who had been in the job for around six months. Evaluations ran Outstanding, Exceeds Requirements, Meets Requirements and Unsatisfactory. He was quite nervous in going over my record and complimented me since I was recently named manager of the year for the second year in a row. When it came to my final rating, he said "Lionel, you've done a great job so I'm evaluating you exceeds requirements". My reply was: "In other words you're telling me that no manager in this district is being evaluated Outstanding?" At that he reached in his bottom drawer and threw some antacid tablets in his mouth. "No, I can't say that, however you know evaluation ratings are confidential". I told him that ratings are as confidential as this morning's headlines and if he would like, I could name the managers who received those ratings. He got so nervous I thought he was going to have a heart attack. From my dealings with him, I felt he would be fair if he had his way. However, I couldn't help feeling that he was instructed as to what my evaluation should be.

Something similar happened to my friend, Earl Wilson. As branch manager in one of the offices in Washington, D. C., he made manager of the year. His district manager evaluated him "exceeds requirements" instead of "outstanding". When his boss told him that he was given a fair evaluation as a branch manager, Earl retaliated and said he was given an evaluation as a "black branch manager". Should I have opened door and gone to higher management? Perhaps so, even though I already had the company record for going "open door". What I didn't realize at that time was that bigger confrontations were in my future. Not just with district and regional managers, but with corporate vice presidents and two division presidents.

As previously stated, I've always warned newly hired black salesmen about obeying the company's rules, regardless of what others may do. When I first arrived in Washington in 1962, assigned to the Washington Federal office, I was told how I

86

could save a substantial amount of money in my moving expenses, savings that I would then be able to pocket. It's ok, everyone's doing it, I was told. Sure enough, this was confirmed by others. Can you imagine the hammer that would have been over my head during my many confrontations with management, if I had participated. Even when I took customers to lunch, *I covered myself with receipts. When I was told that I could only apply the amount that is over what I normally spend for my personal lunch, I would mark my expense account: "customers lunch...6.50 my lunch 6.50 less 3.50 personal...charging IBM 3.00 for my lunch.* Am I being psychotic? I have memorandums from my boss to administration, requesting copies of my personal expense accounts. Counting mileage, my expenses rarely ran over thirty dollars a week. And my branch was doing a multi-million dollar business.

In the late spring of 1970, following two fantastic performances by the Cherry Hill branch, I received a call from the regional manager. (The region covered the eastern third of the country.) He wanted me to take over the branch office in Baltimore, Maryland. The Baltimore branch was three times the size of Cherry Hill. Cherry Hill did not warrant a marketing manager to assist me. (That is, until I was replaced. The new branch manager was assigned a marketing manager). The Baltimore branch had three marketing managers reporting to the branch manager. Since my arrival, Cherry Hill had doubled its size and multiplied the revenue it produced many times over. Of the original six representatives, I was able to have one promoted into management. Considering everything, The Cherry Hill office was now a pretty good office to manage. I asked the Regional Manager to give me time to think about it. What surprised me was that my wife was elated. She made some good friends when we lived in the District of Columbia and Baltimore was just 45 minutes away. So after six years, I decided to accept the move to Baltimore. Before accepting, one of the senior salesmen, who I had confided in, invited me to lunch and tried his best to talk me out of it.

The Cherry Hill staff gave me a great farewell party which I'll always remember. I saluted them for being the top sales force in the district and thanked them "for making me look good". It was sad to leave, not only an excellent staff, but good friends.

CHAPTER IX

"BALTIMORE - ANOTHER CAMPAIGN?"

I was installed as Branch Manager of the Baltimore office in June, 1970. Arriving in Baltimore, my hope, especially after the success's achieved by the Cherry Hill office during my tenure, was that the sniping by higher management would abate and I would be able to concentrate all my energies to building the business in Baltimore. Unfortunately, it was not to be. I would continue to enjoy a good working relationship with those I worked with, as was the case in Cherry Hill, but not with my superiors. I was soon to learn that being assigned to a much larger branch perhaps gave some of my superiors the idea that I presented a much larger target. One that was easier to hit.

The present manager of Baltimore was being promoted to manager of our divisions sales school in Dallas, Texas. While his promotion was being announced in Dallas, my announcement was taking place in Baltimore. After the meeting, the Regional Manager suggested that I had a lot of cleaning up to do. He felt that many in Baltimore's sales force shouldn't be in the business. Thanking him for his suggestions (remembering old advise from the Vice President of Sales) I said that I intended to familiarize myself with the operations before making any decisions. As for those thought to have problems, I wanted to hear their side.

For the next two months I listened, asking mostly probing questions when something said wasn't clear. I learned a lot, enough to start making decisions. One sales representative who was totally demoralized and expecting to be released when I arrived, performed so well he was promoted within two years. Another,who had to be read the riot act but was extremely talented, eventually became a division director. The few I eventually released, left with no bad feelings. What I

89

emphasized to the marketing managers was that if anyone can't perform, we may have to take away their job but let's make certain we don't take away their pride. I encouraged my managers to concentrate on the good points an individual had before bringing up what they considered their shortcomings. When you first compliment someone, their more apt to feel that you're trying to be fair and tend to be more receptive to criticism. Frequently, I used to hear from individuals I had to release from the business. For the most part, they were doing well. Why? I always tried to pump them up, citing individuals who became successful after switching careers.

I remember one individual came into my office expecting to be fired, and before I could say anything, told me he was a failure. I asked him in what? He said, "this business". Because he failed in one business career out of thousands of others, he assumed he was a failure. I then started naming different professions that I would fail in and he soon got my point. He finally admitted that he always wanted to get into home construction and that he liked using his hands to create. He always thanked me for renewing his self-confidence and felt that we did him a favor by showing him he was playing in the wrong ballfield.

Maryland, though considered a northern state, practiced segregation for many years, somewhat similar to its southern neighbors. Recent years had seen some changes in that pattern. Like many cities in the northeast, the flight was to the suburbs, leaving the inner city to blacks and many blue collar ethnic communities that apparently decided to stay put. Our office was in Towson, Maryland, just outside the city limits. The other division branches of IBM were located in downtown Baltimore, in the center of the business district. Before my arrival, approval was given to select a site for a new building that would consolidate all the Baltimore divisions. In order to receive approval by corporate headquarters, all branch managers involved had to appprove the new location. Eventually, when plans were almost formulated for a new location, I was asked to agree to a decision to construct the new building in the suburbs of Baltimore. (The other Divisional Branch Managers had concurred) I had been in the area long enough to observe the rapid deterioration of downtown Baltimore. Many businesses had fled to the suburbs and most of those left were either planning or considering leaving. It was the same pattern of deterioration that just about destroyed my birthplace, Newark, New Jersey. I refused to sign off, with the recommendation that we should stay and construct in downtown Baltimore. Without unanimous approval of all branch managers, plans had to be put on hold. I didn't realize the turmoil my decision had started until I received a call that Bart Steven's, the president of my division, office products, was coming to Baltimore to see me.

Bart Stevens had been second in command to our recently retired president, Gordon Moodie. No, Gordon wasn't forced to retire for installing me as IBM's first black branch manager. But the word passed through the black network was that he had gone too far in espousing the ideas of the civil rights movement. Where Gordon was a great listener, Bart was a great talker. When he arrived, we discussed the Baltimore branch, business potential and personnel, but not my veto of the move to the suburbs. That evening, we did have a lively discussion regarding IBM's appointment of a black woman,Patricia Harris, a prominent attorney and former Dean of Howard University's Law school, to IBM's Board of Directors. Being the first black member of IBM's board, he asked me if this met with the approval of the black community. I knew my answer wasn't going to be the one he was looking for, but I thought, "what the hell, I'm already on the s--t list, so I replied: "Bart, before I answer directly, I want to emphasize that I'm not questioning the qualifications of Ms. Harris to sit on IBM's board. I'm also not questioning the appointment of a black woman to the board. What I am questioning is the pattern that corporations are taking in appointing black board members. Take a look at the black appointee's to the boards of major corporations and you'll find that the great majority are black women. In fact (the year is 1971), I can't name one black man who is on the board of a major corporation. As there are many highly qualified black women in the business world, there are also many highly qualified black men. So don't interpret my words as disparaging

91

to those black women who have been appointed. After all both black women and men have been going through hell together. One associate in IBM, while praising the appointment of Mrs. Harris to IBM's board, was critical of the pattern being set by major corporations, describing it as another attempt by the white man to castrate the black man." He followed his remarks by stating that IBM got double credit, one for naming a woman and one for naming a black.

I was surprised that Bart didn't reply because he wasn't known to hold back on his opinions. By his silence I sensed that my "honest opinion" may not have hit the right key. Nevertheless, I felt better by being truthful and letting it all out.

While driving Bart to the airport the next afternoon to catch his plane, he finally brought up the "branch office location" subject. Bart wanted to know why I objected, considering the fact that most businesses were moving out of the city, cost per square foot would be cheaper, most of our employee's now live in the suburbs, and various other reasons. When Bart finished what he probably thought was a convincing "sales Pitch",I replied:

"Bart, the cities are dying throughout the country because businesses are leaving for the suburbs. The cities are like the core of an apple and if the core rots, it soon envelops the entire apple, which includes the suburbs. IBM is one of the largest and most successful corporations in this country. I believe the corporation, besides having a business obligation to its stockholders, also has a moral obligation to the country. We've never followed, we always led. I think it would be a big mistake to follow those who have fled. I believe we have a moral obligation to lead.. By building in the city, we would act as leaders, and strong leaders quickly gather followers. I believe other companies would follow our example and a renaissance will occur in downtown Baltimore."

There was no indication from Bart as to whether he accepted my reasons. In fact, I felt that I would be overruled. Imagine my shock, a few weeks later, when word came down that the Chairman of the Board of IBM decided that the building would be erected in downtown Baltimore. And for icing on the cake, he further ordered that no branch office could move from an inner city without his approval. *I also understand that part of the Newark office of IBM was ordered to move back to the city. Bart was always an excellent salesman so with the results, I can only assume that he supported and delivered my message.*

IBM's plans were to build an eleven story building with a parking garage, with an additonal twenty three stories to be built on top of the garage in later years. (The additional stories were added in the early ninety's. Initially, some nearby businesses protested the addition, since the IBM building faced the inner harbor. Their objections were rejected because the IBM Real Estate Division had the foresight to get the approval during the original construction).

When the news came out, Mayor D'Alesandro of Baltimore was so elated he was on television practically every night singing his praises of IBM. The mayor allowed IBM to pick their site and from what I understand, gave the land without cost.

What was amazing is that, within a very short time, other companies started making committments to stay and rebuild. The Rouse Company, the builders of the new city of Columbia, Maryland, rebuilt Baltimore's Inner Harbor with a shopping and entertainment mall. Today, as compared to 1971, downtown Baltimore has become a magnet for businesses, with a new convention center, residents, with the rehabilitation of homes in the area and visitors with the construction of new football and baseball stadiums in the same area IBM was considering abandoning. The IBM building is at the center of the downtown complex, facing Baltimore's inner harbor. With the "high rise" added in the early ninety's, IBM's building stands out like a diamond. IBM's Chairman's decision to lead rather than follow, by building in the inner city, would forge a lasting tribute to IBM for laying the cornerstone that rebuilt Baltimore's inner city and set an example for other cities to follow.

Every few years, IBM sponsors what they describe as "Family Dinners" in different locations. They included the employee and their spouse. Some years after leaving the Baltimore office, I received an invitation for my wife and I to attend a family dinner in Baltimore. The guest speaker was the president of IBM's real estate division-world wide. The main part of his speech was showing slides of IBM buildings, including research laboratories, offices and plants around the world. The very last slide on the screen was Baltimore's IBM building. He began praising everything about the building. Considering my past confrontations with higher management, his closing statement came as a shock: "ladies and gentlemen, the individual responsible for our good fortune, who fought for this location is with us tonight. Lionel Fultz.. Lionel, will you please stand. Let's give him a big hand." After the dinner, he came by and thanked me personally. After a lapse of almost ten years, his recognition of my efforts was greatly appreciated.

My first two years in Baltimore were very challenging. Having three marketing managers who were directly responsible to work with and train their groups, gave me more time to focus on the office's needs and support the needs of the managers and individuals who needed help. There was a lot of talent amongst the sales force, and I felt we should be making better use of those individuals. There had been very little movement as far as promotions go, so this became one of my priorities. Where there's the greatest opportunity for advancement is where you'll find a highly motivated sales force. Within two years, three sales representatives were promoted. Many more were to follow.

I wish I could say that I was as successful in promoting my marketing managers. One manager in particular was Bob Brady. Bob was an outstanding marketing manager who worked hard to make his people do well. Many of those who were recommended for promotion came from his group. Two eventually became directors of IBM. With all his attributes, his shortcoming was the same as mine, "he was a lousy politician". Bob knew this and couldn't change. If we were in a meeting with the district manager listening to his ideas for the business, and Bob disagreed with a particular statement, he would be on his feet in a second. Bob and I would often disagree on certain strategies. He was always well prepared, which made me re-examine my thoughts before rendering a judgement. I owed a lot to Bob. As his manager, I learned a lot and profited from his abilities. Bob

94

could not be rejected for promotion due to his performance. The only answer I seemed to get from my superiors was; "I just don't have that feeling in my gut for him". Bob once jokingly told me; "the Irish mafia in IBM seems to be holding me back"...We both gave a wry smile to his words since Bob is a very proud Irishman from Boston.

In ten and a half years as a branch manager, in Camden and Cherry Hill, I never had a morale problem. In both offices, the volume of business had increased substantially. Three times my offices led the district. When I was assigned as branch manager, both offices had no candidates on the promotion list. In Camden and later in Baltimore with the assistance of my management team, a number of our sales representatives were promoted into management. What's more important, several of those continued up the ranks and have made substantial contributions to the company. Did I ever make mistakes in managing people? Yes, many times. The next question should probably be: "then why didn't you have morale problems?". The answer is simple. When first introducing myself to an employee for the first time, I always let them know that I wasn't perfect and may sometimes make the wrong move. Continuing: "This office can't be successful unless its people are successful. To become successful, we need ideas that will help management make the right decisions to increase our business. I would rather use 10, 20 or 30 minds to come up with those ideas and decisions than just one, which is mine. If I don't accept your idea, then I should explain why. If you disagree with my explanation, then you explain why. The final decision has to be mine, but the idea may be yours and the credit goes to you." I would then explain to them IBM's "open door" policy, where they can always go to my boss with a complaint against me. If they weren't aware, I would tell them about Tom Watson's "wild duck" speech. I also emphasized that if they desired to be a "wild duck", I would not shoot them down as long as they were producing and not violating company rules. My closing statement was that my door was always open, with or without an appointment.This was just my first step to gain their confidence. That , of course, could only be gained by my actions and not just words.

In all my years of management, employee morale was always a high priority. You simply don't give your best if you're not happy. Despite my record, and the accolades received from higher management for my achievements, I was soon to learn that "old wounds never heal", and instead of receiving support from higher management in building the Baltimore office, a huge obstacle was about to be placed in my path.

When I first entered management, the concern of some was that a black manager wouldn't be accepted by the personnel in his office. It is now 1974 and I'm in my 11th year as a branch manager. In those eleven years I had nothing but complete support from those I worked with, both in Cherry Hill and Baltimore. I enjoyed mutual respect even from the few that couldn't make it. Even when business was slow, we had no morale problems. They always knew what was on my mind and they certainly let me know what was on theirs. I supported their efforts and they always supported me. Did some ever get angry with me. Many times. That's why my door was always open. If they proved me wrong, I would admit it and correct the grievance. If they were wrong, I would thank them for showing confidence in me, knowing that I wouldn't penalize anyone for disagreeing. Did I achieve results? No. We, the entire office, worked together to achieve the results. I always gave them the credit for any success that I had. I felt that my relations with other branch managers, for the most part, were good. Some became very good friends and at times offered excellent advice and assistance.

So then, I always asked myself, why? Why the continuous harrassment by higher management? I became a branch manager at age 42. Most of those in my sales class were in management before they were 30. I am now 52 and approaching my 25th year in the business, always hoping that the last battle with higher management has been fought. Since arriving in Baltimore, the office has seen substantial growth. Also, to help enhance IBM's reputation in the community, I involved myself on a voluntary basis with many organizations: "United Way", board member of Keswick Home for Incurables, National Council of Christians and Jews, Morgan State

University Foundation and the Voluntary Council of Maryland". And despite my efforts to build the business and enhance IBM's reputation in the community, I still wondered, why? The "executive interview", meant to be a method of helping management, was constantly used to undermine me, hoping to create morale problems that would destroy my effectiveness as branch manager. This is why I owe a debt to those that I managed, who continually resisted the efforts to knock me down and instead became a defensive barrier against the attacks. Especially the managers who worked with me, Bob Brady, Nancy Chapelle and Gary Helsel, knowing that it would probably kill their chances for promotion. Things had been quiet too long. My district manager's policy was to let you run the office unless problems arose. With his promotion, we received a new manager, who was just the opposite. My philosophy was that a manager builds a company by doing everything possible to assist and develop your most important resource, your people. The experience I went through for the next eighteen months with my new boss indicated that his management style was the opposite of mine. Where I supported if needed, he disparaged. Where I assisted, he attacked. Where I tried to build, he tried to destroy. However, the worst part was that, even after higher management was warned of his actions, not just by me but by other branch managers in the district, higher management refused to act.

February, 1974, the Baltimore office was assigned to District 3, headed by my new boss. Almost immediately, harrassment started. It started in the form of criticism of every decision that I made as branch manager. As a branch manager, you're often presented with different options by your subordinates in achieving certain goals. The final decision is left up to you. Deciding which way to go isn't always the obvious direction for success.

Regardless, you're responsible for your decisions success or failure. Hopefully, you're right most of the time. Of course, you can avoid making mistakes by not making decisions. In that case, you're not running your operation. My new boss wanted justification and documention of practically every decision I made. Whenever branch managers met, this was the main topic in private conversations. He would try to embarrass branch managers at meetings by singling one out to ask: "Mike, a pink letter came out last month No. 36452, regarding the handling of green letters. Please let me know what you thought of the fourth paragraph, item 3A?" If our boss was asked what was on page 5, section 2 of the same letter, I doubt that he would know. From his actions, we could only assume that he wanted to let us know who was in command and how easily he could expose what he considered our deficiencies. At a Manager's meeting in Washington, D.C. in May of 1974, he had a violent outburst in the presence of another district manager and a branch manager. He used a derogatory remark to describe both me and the other branch manager. The host district manager, immediately adjourned the meeting, and everyone dispersed.

I sent a letter to my manager, objecting to his remarks during the meeting. No reply was received.

Instead of a reply, shortly after, I received a 60 second evaluation. The evaluation wasn't good, despite the fact that Baltimore had achieved 100% of quota two years in a row for the first time in over ten years. He refused to discuss the evaluation and simply stated that this was how he felt. I signed the evaluation and wrote on it that a memorandum would follow questioning the entire evaluation.

In August, at a managers meeting in Williamsburg, Virginia, I asked to meet with the regional manager, my manager's boss. He listened but was not sympathetic to anything I had to say. He spent more time discussing the benefits of using an electric razor. (He convinced me. I've used one since)

After that meeting, the harrassment became greater than ever. The Disrict Manager made repeated phone calls to the Baltimore office checking on my whereabouts in such a tone, that everyone who handled the calls became aware of the dissension. Most often he would call every Friday at approximately 5:05 or 5:10 PM. When he made calls with sales representatives, they felt it was his way of demeaning me personally with them.

One rule I insisted on with the marketing managers was that if an individual isn't meeting requirements and not showing improvement, if we must release him, try our best not to take away their pride. We would often encourage them by emphasizing their strengths and simply stating that they might be successful in a different field. This frequently proved true. One of the first salesmen I had to release, entered a different field and from what I learned became a millionaire. I mention this because whenever an individual is released from the business, an exit interview must be conducted by his managers superior. In my case, it meant that my district manager conducted the exit interviews of anyone I released. Many of those I released, often kept in touch with me. This is how I learned he was using exit and executive interviews as a means of hitting back at my operations in Baltimore. His attitude became so hostile that it became readily apparent to most personnel in the Baltimore office. A serious side affect was that it limited managements effectiveness because we were so busy attempting to justify all our actions. His actions against me were so vociferous that it was impossible to hold down the speculation within the office. Though I would deny to our personnel that anything was wrong at the time, many, including managers, offered their support if needed. Nothing else makes the job more worthwhile. What I found hard to understand was why the other branch managers tolerated him. Doing a little investigating with friends in headquarters I learned that he was on a "fast track" for higher positions and considered untouchable.

In January, 1975, my district manager visited the Baltimore office late Friday afternoon and began subjecting me to a battery of questions regarding the operations of Baltimore. He would not listen completely to my answers and constantly interrupted me before I could properly answer. The longer he talked the more he raged.

His actions indicated to me that groundwork was being set to destroy my credibility and cause my removal as branch manager. My only choice if I was to save my position was to fight back. After approximately 20 minutes of his tirade I asked him to "get out of my office because the matter was no longer a meeting but harangue. I didn't explode or raise my voice, but he probably sensed that he'd better leave. Without a word, he grabbed his hat and briefcase and headed for the elevator.

I then called the Vice President of Sales and asked for an appointment. Not long after I hung up, my boss's boss, the regional manager was on the phone. (Apparently my boss had called him from a pay phone in the lobby.) He exchanged greetings and acted as if he was unaware of what happened, so I interrupted the conversation and stated: "I tried to discuss the situation with you, but was completely ignored. In the meantime I've been going through a living hell. I just called the Vice President to set up an appointment to meet with him. I should have done this sooner, because his actions have been debilitating to our operations and affecting our people. I couldn't hold off any longer". His only response was that he would probably hear from his boss, the Vice President of Sales.

During my meeting with the Vice President of Sales, the vibrations I received didn't seem good. So what I put on the table were my boss's actions that were contrary to IBM's policies and the lack of respect that he showed for the individual. I then suggested that before he decided one way or the other, that he speak with the other branch managers in the district to get their opinion.

He did talk to the other branch managers and informed me that I was absolutely right in every respect and that their statements were so similar, it almost appeared as if it was rehearsed. His next statement came as a shock. "I would like you to continue to work with your manager in order to help him turn around." I couldn't believe it. Anyone else would have been crucified. Did they think I should give him another chance to shoot me down since he missed the target the first time? I then reminded him that he was asking me to deal with a boss who even sent a letter to one of my marketing managers that was intended to undermine me. I then suggested that he think over his decision and let me know. If he insisted on maintaining a position that to me was untenable, I would have to go "open door".

By this time, I had lost complete faith in getting a fair hearing in our division. Time and again I was subjected to actions by my superiors that were meant to undermine my efforts to manage an office. Since Gordon Moodie retired, not once did any executive call off the wolves until they discovered that I was holding nothing but aces in my hand. The Vice President of Sales must have sensed that my next stop was at the office of IBM's Chairman of the Board.

On the following Monday morning I received a call from the Administrative Assistant to the president of the division. He told me that the Vice President of Sales had tried to reach me over the weekend in order to inform me that my district manager was being transferred in three weeks to take over the Philadelphia district.

I was pleased but very disappointed. That call told me that the whole problem had moved up to the presidents office. What is more serious is that if they thought he was right and I was wrong, why worry about my going to the chairman's office? After all, if I was sure to fail, they could show me the nearest exit. By moving him into a lateral position, they knew I had a case but still wanted to protect him. (Obviously, a GOB...good ole boy). Not too long after, I heard that he was removed from his position as district manager in Philadelphia. A branch manager from the district informed me that a situation occurred in a branch that required certain steps be taken by the regional manager and reported to the chairmans office before any action could be taken to release a senior salesman. As I was told, the regional manager was assured by the district manager, that those steps required by the Chairman had been taken. The branch manager told me that the party who was released, informed the chairman's office that those steps weren't taken, and the roof blew off. He added that the regional manager was asked by the chairman's office if he knew what was going on in his region.

With my old district manager gone and a new one assigned, and considering the fact that the Baltimore office had the best record in the district for 1975, you would think that my adversaries would put their guns back in their holsters. Well think again. I've heard that when people get frantic, they often don't think straight. The next attack caused me to feel that panic had really set in, because this coming foray against me didn't make any sense at all.

Keep in mind that in the mid-seventies, the Baltimore office was running a multi-million dollar business. Other branch managers, in order to keep their staff motivated, often spent money on awards and outings if certain goals were to be achieved. This included dinners for the award winner and their spouse, monetary awards and prizes such as TV sets. I've never heard of a branch manager being questioned since the money was spent for a good cause. After so many confrontations with my past district managers, it didn't surprise me when I received a memo from my new district manager. It also further confirmed that others had urged him to "keep the heat on".

On July 27, 1976, I received the following memo from my new district manager: "Subject: Business Expenses....Lionel, I have just approved your expense account for the week of 6/11/76, with a charge of $29.00 for customer's lunches. Your charges in this category are way out of line and they are the highest in the district. I will not approve any more expenditures in this category except for unusual situations."

In reply I sent the following memo to my district manager, dated August 4, 1976.: "Your letter dated July 17, 1976. The business item in question was a business related expense in our efforts to get the Baltimore City Government to change their present low bid policy regarding Word Processing. The guest (name on expense account) is a close aid to he Mayor of Baltimore City. I am more concerned about your statement that my expenses are way out of line and are the highest in the district. It is difficult for me to deal with the expense requirements of other offices, but as Branch Manager, I am expected to maintain high level contact in our pursuit of business. Because of my association memberships, I am in frequent contact with many of our customers and individuals who have influence in some of our large accounts. I feel that I should be compensated for all business related expenses but have hesitated to submit some, in the past, due to past criticism regarding this subject. I do feel we have to discuss this in greater detail so that I have a better understanding of what is expected of me regarding business expenses. The following is not related to the above but I feel you should be aware of the situation. As I have mentioned before, I have become very involved in community activities that are related to the betterment of the inner city and the enhancement of economic and educational opportunities for minorities. At the present time, I am a member of the Board of the Morgan State University Foundation. I am also a member of the Voluntary Council on Equal Opportunity which is made up of top business executives throughout the Baltimore community. I am also about to embark on a "adopt a school program" in conjunction with the Greater Baltimore Committee. This program is intended to enhance an innercity school's ability to create an atmosphere or environment of motivation. I feel moral commitment to participate in these and many other activities and I assume IBM encourages such participation. My personal expenses are considerable and it would be helpful to me personally if IBM offered some financial relief if this is at all possible. I feel my participation has helped and is continuing to improve IBM's image in the greater Baltimore area. I would like to discuss this matter with you apart from the subject of this memo."

(I never received a reply.)

During this period I made a special trip to see IBM's CEO, Frank Cary, seeking assistance to develop an MBA program at Morgan State University. The chairman, Frank Cary, approved the largest private donation Morgan State University had ever received. I paid my own travel expenses.

In my seven years at Baltimore, I gave an annual party at my home for employee's and their spouses without submitting an expense account. The following year, 1977, the United Negro College Fund gave me an award for serving as General Chairman of their Maryland campaign. I felt that my efforts contributed towards improving IBM'S image in the greater Baltimore community. My managers never offered to compensate me in any way. My compensation came from the appreciation expressed by community leaders and the organizations that were helped. I never received a reply to my

103

memo or a word of praise from my superiors for my work in the community. Which, I might add, I never let interfere with my business responsibilities. (Baltimore was producing millions of dollars worth of business and all this over a $29.00 expense account)

Should I be prepared for the next assault? I didn't have to wait. Instead of using all of my energies to foster the growth of the Baltimore office, it appears like I'm also defending myself against a vendetta by those who should assist me.

Another problem also cropped up during my discussion with the Vice President of Sales. I complained that I felt Baltimore was assigned too high a quota. He agreed to send one of their top statisticians in headquarters, Charles DeRahm, to investigate our quota assignment. Quota assignment is normally based on installed inventory. Another factor that could change your quota is a large productive account moving in or out of your offices territory. The other factor is the economy. If the economy is down in your area, the district office can reduce your quota.

After a few days, DeRahm couldn't find any discrepancies based on our installed inventory. Years ago, DeRahm once handled the National Security Agency, one of the largest accounts in the area. It was based at Fort Meade, which geographically was in the Baltimore territory. Before my arrival, the sales responsibility was transferred to the Washington Security branch office. The servicing of the equipment was still maintained by Baltimore customer engineers. The way I got the story is that Charley asked what salesman was handling NSA. He recognized the name as a representative in the Washington office. He then discovered that we were being charged, over the years, for NSA's inventory and carrying the Washington office's quota. He also stated, before me and the three marketing managers, that our 1974 quota would have been 11% lower over the years if we weren't charged for NSA's inventory. As a result of this, one of the marketing managers, Bob Ballentine, sent a letter to me, which I forwarded to the Vice President of Sales, requesting retroactive quota reduction. This would mean a substantial amount of money due to the managers since their compensation was based on percent of quota attained. This was

104

rejected with a statement by him that Mr. De'Rahm did not make that statement to us and it did not affect the setting of machine quota's. In other words, the Vice President of Sales was accusing me and the three marketing managers of being liars.   The marketing manager who sent the letter, totally discouraged, soon resigned his management postion and asked to be transferred to a sales representative positon. This was a big loss to our office. Besides losing a very capable and experienced manager, it left us with only one experienced marketing manager since one had recently been promoted.

In World War II, when General Patton's 3rd army first broke though at St. Lo in Normandy, France, even though my unit was a good distance away, we could feel the ground shake with the roar of shells exploding and aerial bombs. I was again beginning to feel the ground shake. Another battle campaign was starting for me in IBM and I had no idea that this one would be the biggest.

CHAPTER X

UNDER FIRE BY THE "BIG GUNS"

The first sortie began. On or about June 11, 1976, the Vice President of Sales called to say he wanted to visit the Baltimore office and conduct some executive interviews. It's very rare for a Vice President to conduct executive interviews in a branch office, unless someone goes "open door" from the branch or there is a serious morale problem that reaches the Division Presidents or Chairman's office. All I can do is "dig a deeper foxhole" until I learn what I'm up against.

I'm now in my 26th year in the business and 12th year as a branch manager, and never had any subordinate go "open door" against me.

As before , many of those that the Vice President interviewed said they were asked leading questions: "What's wrong with the morale in the Baltimore office?" "If you had to rate the morale from 1-10, how would you rate it?" Once again my superiors miscalculated by assuming they could foster a morale problem in our office by intimating through their questioning that my superiors questioned my leadership. Once again they were unaware of the mutual respect I shared with those I managed. Once again, as in the Cherry Hill Branch, those questioned, as they related to me, felt an attempt was being made to use them and were quite upset about the tactics used.

After the interviews, the Vice President said there were a few problems but wouldn't define them. (Now comes the real reason for his visit) The tactic is so obvious to me, that I suspected something was going to be put on the table. Those wielding the power wanted me out. Hint there's a morale problem in your office, to make you a little nervous then make the offer.

IBM divided the country into three regions, Eastern, Midwestern and Western. The Vice President said that

107

corporate was considering the divisions request to establish a fourth region, running from Washington, D.C. to Florida. He asked me if I would consider the position of Regional Personnel Manager if this was approved. I replied that I would consider the offer but would not commit myself until I learned more about the job.

July 15, I was called to Headquarters to see the Vice President of Sales. Instead of a regional job, he offered me a personnel program managers position, which was much lower than my present position. He denied making any other offer. Once again, the Vice President of Sales is calling me a liar, even though he described the geographic makeup of the new region to me in our previous meeting.

Usually executive interviews are conducted once a year. It's now October, and so many executive interviews have been conducted in Baltimore this year that I've lost count. The Baltimore office is now reporting to the Washington, D.C. district office, and assigned a new district manager.

My new District Manager was a protege and close friend of my first district manager when I managed the Camden branch. For a while he worked as an assistant to the District Manager and eventually became branch manager in the Trenton office, which abutted the Cherry Hill office that I managed. In a few large cities, where they had several branch offices, the division established market support centers, having the branch managers reporting to the center manager. This cut into the branch managers power and wasn't too welcomed by them. With just two branches covering the southern two thirds of the state, it didn't make any sense having a market support center in the lower two-thirds of New Jersey. What it would accomplish would be to cut my power when I was Branch Manager of the Cherry Hill office. At the time, the District Manager informed me that he was making Trenton and Cherry Hill a Market support center with the Trenton manager in charge. Since there was no good business reason for the move, it was clear to me what he was trying to do. I said that if that's the case, I was going to see the division president, Gordon Moodie. Guess what? The whole thing was immediately dropped.

108

Since our first meeting years ago when he was assistant to my first District Manager, my new boss was never friendly. At branch manager meetings, before his promotion, he never accepted a gesture on my part to be friends. I could only assume that my conflicts with his boss had something to do with his attitude. Now, in October, 1976, he's my boss and next in line to conduct executive interviews in the Baltimore office.

The pattern remained the same as they were going back to my old Cherry Hill office. Interviews conducted, leading questions asked, fishing for problems, with the conclusion that I may have some problems but they can't be defined. And, as usual, those interviewed, wondering what's going on. Is it another fishing expedition? He said he would get back to me, when I asked what the negative comments were. This never happened.

On October 28, my new boss asked if I would consider an executive loan position if one became available. I said I was happy doing my present job but would consider a significant position if the terms were suitable. A few weeks later, I received a call to be interviewed by a Mr. Don Doll for a position in Washington, D. C.The position was insignificant and Mr. Doll couldn't understand why they would send someone in my position to interview for the job.

It wasn't long before the storm clouds started gathering once again. My detractors, it appeared, came up with what they may have considered a brilliant idea. Every time they came at me in the past, they lost. Simply because they never had their facts straight and misjudged the loyalty of those who I managed and worked with. Their new idea to "spring the trap" on me bordered on the ridiculous as events proved.

A few months before, our regional manager had been replaced. The new Regional Manager was the former administrative assistant to the Division President. As Regional Manager, he was the highest ranked black in the division. On December 20, 1976, I received a call from my boss, stating that the new Regional Manager would like to see me in his office on December 23, in Harrison, New York. My District Manager said that he was going to offer me another position in the Executive loan program. He added that it was a significant position and I should be very interested in.

Anyone would think that I would be highly optimistic since for the first time I'm meeting with someone in higher management who happens to be black. Having dodged so many arrows in the past, I felt no sense of elation but did feel that perhaps here is someone that will at least listen to my side of the story and judge for himself. At the time, little did I realize that this meeting will spark one of the biggest confrontations of my career.

I arrived in Connecticut the night before the meeting and spent the night with my good friend, Earl Wilson and his family. Earl was now working with IBM's World Trade Corporation and trying to get an assignment to Paris, France. My commute wasn't too far the next morning. I arrived at the Regional Manager's office on time and was soon escorted into his office.

During the first one and a half hours, it was my impression that I was being reminded of the power of his office. In practically all my meetings with IBM executives, they always held calls and got right down to business. When he wasn't on the phone, the Regional Manager would excuse himself while he made a call and started barking orders. I started to get annoyed at what I considered bad manners but on second thought dismissed his actions as a personality trait. He finally got down to business.

Once again, as with others, he knew very little information about the job he was offering and from what he knew, it did not appear to be a very significant position. I told him that I would rather hold up any decision until he found out more information about the position. At this point, he asked me if there was anything else I would be interested in doing so that I could take a year's leave from the business. (What could be more clear that their purpose is to get rid of me) Then came what he thought would be the knockout punch. Regional Manager: "your District Manager informed me that you are having problems in the Baltimore office and Baltimore was one of the offices that never fully assigned its quota during 1976. Considering your present position, this might be a good time to make a change". In the infantry the word was that if they wanted to learn the enemy's position, send the least trained troops up front. They were called cannon fodder. Looking back, I now feel that the Regional Manager was being used. He knew nothing about my record, my past confrontations and my past refusals to throw up the white flag. He was totally misinformed and probably concluded that leading the attack on me would really put him in good stead. What he should have known is that many others had failed, with some walking away with damaged careers. When your under attack, you have only two choices, surrender or defend yourself.

In the discussion that followed, I accused the Regional Manager of attempting to undermine my position, since he admitted sending my boss into Baltimore for the executive interviews. I also informed him that, once again, sales representatives informed me that they were asked leading questions, i.e.: "What's wrong with the sales programs in Baltimore?" "Are you content with your compensation and why didn't you complain?" I reminded him of the reasons quota was unassigned and stated that the timing for executive interviews could not have been more inappropriate, especially since no complaints had been received from any personnel in Baltimore. I told him that once again, I was being harrassed and felt his statements were intimidating and demeaning and not in conformity with IBM's policies.

I summarized my statements by stating that in my twelve years as a branch manager, IBM has never received a letter from any personnel accusing me of unfair practices. I also reminded him that as a branch manager, I had led the district three times, most recently last year. I added that if he had taken time to compare my record in Baltimore during the past six years with the six years prior to my coming, he would have recognized a great improvement, not only in the sales record but in the personnel we have developed and promoted into management. I told him that this was the ninth time,since becoming a branch manager, that executive interviews were used in an attempt to undermine me. I told him that my protests within the division have always brought only temporary solace and that I did not intend to be a duck in a shooting gallery for him or anyone else

111

any longer and intended to take my case to the Chairman of the Board.

Without prolonging the discussion, I grabbed my hat and coat and headed for the elevator. Being an extremely cold day, I started my engine and was waiting for the car to warm up when the Regional Manager appeared in his shirt sleeves and began pleading with me to return and discuss the matter further. I didn't even bother replying and just took off for Maryland.

During my career, every time time I acceded to a request not to carry my case higher up, it only provided my opponents time to regroup and plan a new way to try to bring me down.

It was almost a five hour drive to return home to Columbia, Maryland. It gave me time to consider everything that had happened since I was promoted to branch manager. As T. G. always said, "being the first is bad enough. But when you prove they're wrong by not only doing a good job but insisting that you're doing it when they're trying to prove you're not, you only inflame a prejudiced mind. Prove their point, and you'll probably end up with a secure position for the rest of your working days with the company".

Arriving home , I immediately typed a brief letter to the Chairman of the Board, Frank Cary, requesting a meeting. In a few words I simply stated that considering the actions that have been taken against me since my promotion to branch manager, I can only conclude that there is a conspiracy against me. I was surprised how soon I got an appointment. A reservation was made for me at a motel in Armonk, New York, the location of IBM's World headquarters.

Chapter XI

Meeting with IBM's C.E.O.

Soon after I arrived Sunday evening in Armonk, N. Y., a huge snowstorm started. By the next morning, many were snowed in. I soon received a phone call from the chairman's office informing me that he wasn't able to get in and rescheduled the meeting for Tuesday morning.

In that meeting, rather than getting into a long "blow by blow" account of everything that had happened, *I simply stated that management, despite my record, has constantly harrassed and made attempts to undermine me. I then showed him copies of several letters undermining me that had been sent to people reporting to me. One came from a district manager. After reading the letters, he exploded: "We've got some of the dumbest district manager's I've ever seen".*

Being a veteran at "open doors", I was familiar with the procedure. Usually they assign an executive to conduct the investigation. What surprised me is that he called in his executive assistant, George Conrades, and ordered him to conduct the investigation. (The chairman's executive assistant is usually on the fast tract to reach one of the top corporate positions]. With Conrades, I spent a good part of the day describing not everything, but the key episodes, from the first one with my district manager in Camden New Jersey, to the latest with the Regional Manager. From what I later learned, George personally interviewed everyone I named. He informed me that one former district manager, who was presently assigned to a staff position in division headquarters, made the mistake of chewing him out. I should mention at this point that in defending myself whenever I went open door, I always used my record, not my race. Considering the hell I was catching, I didn't have to. The actions clearly reflect their cause.

113

The investigation took several weeks. I returned to Armonk and before meeting with the Chairman, I first met with George Conrades. Everything I stated was verified and, without naming the person, he was very critical of some of those interviewed. He added that the only criticism that some made of me was that "I had an explosive temper". I agreed to this if its meaning was that I was quick to react when I had had enough.

I learned long before I came to IBM that you can't communicate by screaming or shouting. Years ago, while selling in Chicago, I forgot a committment I had made to the president of a small insurance company. When I approached his secretary, she warned me that he was really fuming and she was right. When I walked into his office, he told me to close the door because he didn't want to disturb his secretary, and to sit down...At that, I started to turn around and asked him if he would excuse me for a minute. He shouted "Where the hell are you going, I haven't even started with you".. I replied: "I'm going down to the trunk of my car to get a baseball bat. I figured you would want to use it on me". Magically, it calmed him down. I still got chewed out, but not thrown out. He remained a customer,

After meeting with the chairman of the board, Frank Cary, during which he reiterated the conclusions his executive assistant, George Conrades had arrived at, I returned to Baltimore. Before leaving, he thanked me for bringing the matter to his attention and assured me that my concerns would be taken care of. He also invited me to call him direct, if I felt it necessary, in the future. Such a statement coming from the chief executive officer would make any observer think that my problems were over and the attack would abate. I soon found out that it was wishful thinking on my part. My detractors apparently regrouped and developed a new method of attack. This one was a full blown attack and came several months after my last visit with the chairman.

I had recently lost two of my marketing managers. Bob Ballentine, who had written the letter to the Vice President of Sales asking that he be compensated for the overassignment of quota, asked to be transferred back as a sales representative in

Washington, D. C. He wasn't too happy about the Vice President's rejection of his request. What really upset him was his statement that DeRahm never made the "overassigned quota" statement to me and the marketing managers. Since the Vice President wasn't present when the statement was made in our office, the only person who could refute us was DeRahm. He never quoted DeRahm, just that the statement wasn't made. Just before he left the other marketing manager, Wally Graham, was promoted to a staff position in headquarters.

Any applicant for the vacant marketing manager positions had to come through my District Manager. He sent me a string of applicants that I didn't feel were qualified and had to reject. I felt that I was not being sent the most qualified applicants but after many disappointing interviews, I finally approved an applicant who I felt did not meet all my desires but was the best of the lot. It was my hope that he could develop into a good manager with proper guidance.

At the time the branches were going through a coding procedure of all our data. This had to be done after hours in order to meet a deadline. After interviewing another string of applicants to fill the 3rd marketing manager position, those sent by my District Manager definitely did not meet my requirements. A couple of those interviewed even expressed surprise that they were recommended for promotion. After many frustrating interviews that took a considerable amount of time and recognizing that my district manager was not going to send me the better qualified candidates, I picked the best of the lot.

Not long after my visit with the chairman, here we were with one very capable marketing manager, Bob Brady, one fairly new and becoming acclimated to the position, and one new to the job. I couldn't pull the marketing managers out of the field during the day to work on the re-coding, so this had to be done after hours.

Soon after we got started, I began having problems with my vision. I had to go in for surgery to repair a torn retina. Bob Brady, when told of my problem, quickly volunteered to handle the project and assured me that he, with the assistance of the new marketing managers could complete the job on time. Having complete confidence in Brady and knowing he would let me know if any problems developed, I turned the task over to him. I also informed the new managers of my inability to work on the coding due to my vision problems.

Weeks later, my District Manager had the newer marketing managers in the district's branches report to his offices for an orientation session. When executive interviews are going to be conducted, the branch managers are always notified in advance. Since the new marketing managers were in the district office for an orientation session, I was later informed that the District Manager invited the two new marketing managers from Baltimore into his office for what he described as a "get acquainted session. Since I wasn't notified beforehand that it would be an "Executive Interview", a different description had to be used but the intent was the same as many past "Executive Interviews". Once again, my adversary's had recouped and obviously devised another plan that they felt would cause me to "walk the plank".

Soon after the session ended in Washington, I received a call that my District Manager wanted me to report to his office in Washington, D. C. ASAP. His greeting was the same as always; very cold and abrupt. Though he knew of my hospitalization, he made no queries as to how I was feeling. He immediately tore into me, saying that I had serious problems in Baltimore. He said that the new marketing managers said I was not assisting them in re-coding the branch's records and I was letting Bob Brady run the office. His mind was set and I could see that it would be futile to try to defend myself. By making these charges, this gave him an "open door" to interrogate anyone in the Baltimore office, often with the purpose of creating problems.

I was stunned and also reminded of a statement that the Chairman's executive assistant, George Conrades, made to me. Conrades: "When I interviewed your District Manager, he said that he really liked you". I replied: "A friend helps, not undermines you, as was reported to me by some of the sales representatives who he interviewed. He has never complimented me for any successes the office accomplished and rejected any gesture of friendship or cooperation on my part." I could have added many acts on his part that I could only interpret as an intense dislike for me, personally. But I felt my point was made and felt pressing the issue served no purpose. My first district manager when I was Branch Manager in Camden, New Jersey, was my present manager's boss at the time. He was also considered my present boss's mentor and good friend. If his feelings were germane to my clashes with his old boss, then he was just one of the crowd who put me on their S list because of that episode.

On previous executive interviews, they couldn't get those I worked with in the Baltimore office to turn against me, so now their using two new arrivals, who were probably too intimidated to go against any leading question asked. When he finished castigating me, I made only one statement: "once again you've reached a verdict without first questioning me". I picked up my briefcase and left.

I started to go to the nearest phone booth to call the Chairman's office. But I decided to give myself a couple of hours to make certain I was doing the right thing. I drove back to my office in Baltimore, and after taking a few calls that were waiting for me, called George Conrades at the Chairman's office. I explained to him what had happened and asked for an appointment to see Frank Cary, Chairman and C.E.O. of IBM.

From his voice, I could tell George was upset. He said he would get right back. The next morning George Conrades called and said that Mr. Cary asked our Division President to look into the matter and report back to him. Our new Division President had replaced Bart Stevens, who was promoted to Corporate Headquaters.

The events that were about to occur left me no choice, fight back or jump off the cliff. They were getting ready to push me to the edge. Before I was defending myself against Colonel's and had no idea that I would soon be up against General's, i.e., two Division Presidents.

CHAPTER XII

AGAINST THE WALL

Within an hour I received a call from the Division President's administrative assistant. He named his Administrative Assistant to conduct the investigation and he wanted to know when he could come to see me. The administrative assistant recently worked for my boss's boss, the Regional Manager who led the most recent fiasco against me. I assumed that the Regional Manager had to recommend him for promotion to the Division Presidents office. I informed him that his recent boss was a key player in my charges and asked if he was aware of it. I also added that if he felt it would not conflict with his investigation, I would have no objection. He admitted that he hadn't thought of the conflict and would get back to me.

Within minutes, the phone rang. Picking up the phone a voice blasted out: "This is (the Division President) Who the hell do you think you are questioning my integrity?" I was blasted for at least three minutes. Without giving me a chance to reply, he then said he was assigning the President of the Real Estate division to conduct the investigation and slammed down the phone. This was the person who was to receive the facts regarding my charges and make the recommendation to the Chairman of the Board.

When the 101st Airborne was surrounded at Bastogne during world war II, they had no choice but to fight back. I had no other choice. Now a corporate Vice President and Division President joined the many others who had me on their enemy's list.

The following week I was told to report to my District Managers office in Washington, D. C. to meet with the president of the real estate division who was conducting the investigation. I arrived on time for my appointment but was kept waiting for almost an hour. After being escorted to a small office by a staff

119

member, the door was closed behind me. For almost an hour I sat by myself, listening to loud laughing by my boss, the District Manager and I was soon to learn, the investigator, the president of IBM's Real Estate division.

He finally walked into the office where I was waiting and closed the door behind him. He had a manila file in his hand, filled with papers. Without a hello or greeting me in any way, he took off: "I've been reviewing this file and I've got a few things to say to you". He proceeded to blast me to the point where I was wondering if he walked into the wrong room. It was what I considered gross intimidation. I guess his actions were supposed to cower me to the point where I just rolled over and died. The way he ranted you would think I had planned the bombing of Pearl Harbor. He never questioned me. He just accused. Everything he accused me of was based on someone's opinion, which all boiled down to, IN MY OPINION,: "You're a smart ass and you better back down". I just listened. I didn't react in any way. When he finished raging, I left. He would soon discover that what he thought he muzzled wasn't a pigeon, but a bear, and a black one at that. Once again, I returned home to prepare my counter attack.

Within two weeks, I was ordered to report to the division headquarters in Franklin Lakes, New Jersey. I was to report to the office of the President of the Real Estate Division, who conducted the investigation, at 11:00 am, and the division president, at 12:30. I was informed that the investigation was complete and I was to hear their conclusions. Up to that time, not one word was heard from or asked of me in my defense..

Within our division there were what we called "moles". They were people who would "butter up" to you, as a good buddy would do, to find out what was happening. Any information gained, which was usually given in confidence, went to his boss. This preserved the "moles" job and kept him in favor with the brass.

The one thing those who used the moles didn't know was that a few of us knew who they were. During World War II, England made good use of the Moles that Germany planted in England. They were fed misleading information that misled the enemy as to where the D Day landing was to take place. My tactic was to do just the opposite. I knew they were ready to throw the book at me. The investigator wasn't fed the most crucial information, "that its not my nature to cower when under attack". I intended to feed the mole my plan of attack.

I arrived at Franklin Lakes at 10:00am, an hour early. I called the "mole's " office and told him that I was a little early for some meetings and since we hadn't seen each other for some time, could he meet me in the cafeteria for coffee. Naturally he asked who I was meeting with, so when I told him, he made a "bee" line to the cafeteria. After exchanging pleasantries, he said he was curious as to why I was meeting with "top brass". After a few more prying questions, I started to in "strict confidence". tell him about recent events. I told him that I intended to fight them right up to the chairman's office, and if that didn't succeed, Congressman Bill Clay of Missouri, who was informed of my conflict, was ready to ask the entire Congressional Black Caucus to intercede in my behalf. Observing the "mole", I never saw anyone drink their coffee so fast, apologize and explain that he almost forgot an appointment as he raced away.

At 11:00 I was escorted into my first meeting with the investigator, the President of the Real Estate Division. I could tell he already got the word. In a much calmer voice, as compared to our first meeting, he said he wanted to review the results of his investigation with me. I told him that I wasn't interested in hearing the results of any report where I wasn't allowed to give any input. I continued: "As far as I'm concerned, your investigation was no different than one being conducted by the Gestapo, so I'm not interested. I picked up my briefcase and walked out, without saying goodbye.

I had plenty of time before my appointment with the division president, so I went to the cafeteria for lunch. I arrived on time for my appointment and was immediately escorted into the presidents office..

Once again, there was no raving as during his phone call, but a pleasant greeting. He complained that his leg was giving him trouble and he had to see a doctor. I sat there and waited. I felt he got the message regarding my last meeting and the report from the mole. He finally said that he got word that I walked out of my last meeting. In a calm voice, I replied: "this whole investigation is a farce. The first words I hear from the person who is to pass judgement are opinions against me even before the investigation has started. As I said to the investigator a little over an hour ago, I'm not interested in listening to any report that I wasn't allowed to give input to in any way. As far as I'm concerned, you can do whatever you want to with that report, but if you think you're going to tar and feather me in the town square without a fight, you're mistaken."

As I purposely paused, he lifted up a report that must have been at least 1 1/2 inches thick, and threw it in the thrash basket, commenting that it was staying there. He continued: "Lionel, I wasn't aware of how much you've contributed to the Corporation and how you were awarded the Outstanding Contribution Award. As far as I'm concerned, you can run the Baltimore office as long as you want to. If you're not satisfied with your managers, you can move them out. You tell me what you want to do."

I replied that I was too annoyed to make any decisions at this time. I was returning to Maryland to take time to think things over. It was a very short meeting. It took me four hours to return home. When I walked in the door, my wife told me that the Division President had called several times to see if I had arrived.

During my entire career with IBM I purposely shielded my family from the constant turmoil I was going through. I felt it would have been more difficult for me if my family had to live with the constant and deliberate attempts to destroy my career. Besides my friend and mentor, T. G., only a very few had any idea what I was going through. One friend I have to mention, because once we got to know each other in the late-sixties, he was always there when the walls were closing in and was always ready to join the battle if his assistance was needed. He often indicated that if they're going to shoot my friend down, they will have to take me with him. It didn't start that way.

122

CHAPTER XIII

EARL WILSON - A FRIEND OF THE OPPRESSED

In the late sixties, while still managing the Cherry Hill branch office, I picked up the phone and here's what I heard. "Hey brother, this is Earl Wilson. You know I've just been appointed manager of equal opportunity for the division and we brother's have to get together..." I interrupted... "Who are you? I have no brother in the business, and hung up". Would you believe that after that initial meeting, he became one of my closest and trusted friends.

My first "face to face" meeting with Earl occured in 1967. Our office had moved from Camden to Cherry Hill, New Jersey. Earl was meeting with a group of managers in Philadelphia and we had arranged to meet at a restaurant in Cherry Hill, following his meeting. I almost immediately sensed why Earl's first manager in St. Louis, Ship Atwater, was so impressed with him at their first meeting. If you've ever met anyone that radiates enthusiasm and a strong desire to face the issues, then that person best describes Earl. I admired this trait in Earl, but I cautioned him that he is now in the business world so he's got to be careful not to expose his hand until all the cards are on the table.

Having been thru so many battles with management in IBM and knowing that I could still be a target, I still didn't let my guard down. After all, this was my first meeting with Earl, and what if he turns out to be what black's consider an Uncle Tom. That feeling didn't stay with me as I listened to Earl during our first meeting. In fact, the longer I listened I began to wonder if those people in headquarters realized the type of person they had placed in the position. As it turned out Earl was not only a great crusader, but one of the greatest. In fact, he crusaded so much that many of those who targeted me in the past, started worrying about him and thus took some of the pressure off of me.

I also discovered that Earl was the Captain in the Airborne that the branch manager in St. Louis, in 1963, was so impressed with but was hesitant to hire because "he didn't sound like us"..Well, he hired him, and Earl did a great sales job in a territory that wasn't considered productive.

Starting with my cross-country tour in 1963, IBM began hiring quite a few blacks, mostly in sales, but also in administration and customer engineering. As I once professed in my daily memorandums to corporate while on my special assignment, "Recruiting the top blacks off these campuses means that in most cases these individuals have the knowledge and desire to advance. If in the future, obstacles are placed in their way, then the company is in trouble as far as providing opportunities for blacks is concerned." It didn't take long before problems were starting to occur. I wasn't a bit surprised. When Gordon Moodie refused to accept corporate's request for me to head up their equal opportunity program, they placed an individual in the position, who, I was to soon learn, knew about as much about equal opportunities for blacks as I knew about finding a cure for cancer. And the year was 1963.

Soon after his appointment, the newly named corporate director of equal opportunity, invited me to a meeting in the board room at IBM's world headquarters in New York, to discuss his program. I was surprised to see my friend T. G. Laster was also invited. Included were ten newly hired blacks. Mostly engineers and plant workers. The directors plans were to send these newly hired employee's to campuses of black colleges to recruit new hires. T. G., being a former professor at two black colleges, thought the plan was ridiculous. He stated, during the meeting, that sending these new hires to black college campuses would appear hypocritical. In the past there was absolutely no interest shown by IBM to recruit black students. Now, to show our interest, we send new black recruits who not only didn't know anything about IBM but also weren't too certain about their own future with the company. It would embarrass these new hires who were not qualified to answer

124

questions pertaining to IBM, and they would end up being laughed off the campus. The director wouldn't listen to T. G. and he walked out of the meeting in disgust. I soon excused myself when it became apparent that their plans were made and they really weren't seeking advise, only agreement that they were on the right track.

Not too long after the meeting, several of the recruits attending the meeting called me in Washington. They were laughed off the campuses according to the calls I received. One told me that he was accused by the students of being a flunky for IBM. Several of them called looking for advice. They didn't want to lose their job, but felt awkward in their assignment.

The president of our division, Gordon Moodie, apparently didn't want to make the same mistake. With increasing racial problems in our division, Gordon Moodie, President of our division, made Earl Wilson our first Equal Opportunity manager. If more blacks had to be hired, Earl initiated programs that brought more into the business. Some complained that our testing was unfair, so Earl proved they were right with the famous "chitterling test", published in the New Republic in 1967. The test proved that many questions in our tests were linked to environments that blacks weren't exposed to in those days. As an example, back in 1963, how many blacks could tell you what a birdie was? Very few, if any, knew it was a term associated with golf.   The "Chitterling" test was simply developed to relate to the black environment and the point was made as white managers, not familiar with the black environment, took the chitterling test and failed.

While manager of equal opportunity, Earl was responsible for greatly accelerating the hiring of black employee's in the Office Products Division of IBM. He also was responsible for pressuring management to promote more blacks into management.   Amongst blacks, there used to be a saying that the best way for a black to retain a position as "Equal Opportunity Manager" in Corporate America, was to hinder the program by doing only what you were told to do by higher management. And, of course, the best way to get out of the job, was to do a good job. Earl not only did an outstanding job, he

125

angered those who opposed what he was doing because of his great successes. Sound familiar?

Several years later, Gordon Moodie, the president of our division, and the one responsible for placing me as IBM's first black branch manager, gave the keynote speech at our 100 per cent club in Miami. It was the first club after the assassination of Martin Luther King. Considering the time,place and especially the audience, his speech was very courageous. It called for greater tolerance and echoed many of the thoughts of Rev. King.

Needless to say, many in the audience were stunned. There were still many problems throughout the country regarding school desegregation and discrimination in employment. His speech replaced what is normally one that concerns the company's business. The black attendee's were pleasantly surprised, but from their own experiences in life. sensed what could happen to anyone that "strayed from the crowd".

Not long after, Gordon Moodie took an early retirement. I would guess that he was in his early fifties and appeared to be in excellent health.   Plus, the divisions business, under his leadership, was booming. Even though Gordon left gracefully with no recriminations, most black employee's felt he paid the price for "telling it like it is". Years later, Gordon asked me if the word was that he was forced out because of his speech. I said that practically everyone I talked to thought it was the reason. Gordon replied that he had gone as far as he could in the business and left on his own. As much as I learned to respect Gordon, I can only say that if he gave his word not to reveal the circumstances, he never would.

I also felt that Earl Wilson's close association with Gordon, while he was Equal Opportunity Manager, molded many of Gordon's thoughts regarding civil rights.

After leaving his Equal Opportunity position, Earl returned to sales management. As a sales manager, he quickly gained many honors including Manager of the year, Golden Circle and National Manager of the year. After leaving his Washington branch, Earl managed to be transferred into IBM's World Trade Corporation. He was based in the United States, but traveled extensively. When a high level marketing position opened in

Paris, Earl went after the job. I later learned that a high official oversea's, upon learning that Earl was Black, tried to sidetrack him, using the same type of diatribe that was used against me to keep me out of "white" accounts back in 1952. The high official not only didn't know what he was talking about, he didn't know Earl. When Earl retaliated, the objections quickly vanished. Earl was responsible for Europe, part of Asia and North Africa. In the five years he was stationed in Paris, his performance was always given the highest rating, "outstanding". Such a performance would usually merit a promotion to 3rd level management or division director. Neither happened. Why? The answer by higher management would probably be: "I just didn't have that gut feeling".

Before Earl retired, he had been evaluted "outstanding" for ten consecutive years. In the thirty four years I was in the business, I never knew anyone who achieved that mark. What is more significant is that Earl is most likely the only one who achieved such a record and never was promoted to what was considered 3rd level management.(A district manager's position was considered 3rd level management). When Earl announced his retirement, Black employee's throughout the country came to his retirement dinner,in White Plains, New York, to express their appreciation for his efforts on their behalf. A special trip to New York was made by the leader of one of the African countries that was assigned to him, in order to personally express their friendship.

Upon his retirement, Earl told me that he intended to return to his home city, St. Louis, to try and help the young people in the inner city who were struggling to survive. Many people talk about what they're going to do and that's all they do, talk. Earl Wilson, since I've known him, has only talked about things he intends to do. And what has he done since returning to St. Louis?

Earl used his own funds to create the "St. Louis Gateway Classic Sports Foundation" a non-profit organization dedicated towards improving the social and economic life in the inner city of St. Louis. In just a few years, with the help of many businesses and executives in St. Louis, his organization has poured hundreds of thousands of dollars into programs that are benefitting underprivileged young people. The annual football classic between two black universities, has drawn huge crowds to St.Louis, with great benefits to the business community. Sports tournaments that include boxing, basketball, track and field and baseball are sponsored by his organization throughout the year. Earl is only one of many blacks IBM hired, who despite outstanding performances, the company failed to take full advantage of their great potential. If you're ever in St. Louis and mention "the St. Louis Gateway Classic Foundation," you always get a smile. For many inner city disadvantaged youths who didn't have hope, Earl Wilson didn't just talk about giving it to them, he gave it to them.

The St.Louis Gateway Classic Foundation which he started with his own personal funds gives everything back to the community. Besides distributing thousands of dinners to the needy during the holiday season, they awarded 20 four year scholarships yearly to disadvantaged youths in the inner city of St. Louis.

Before his retirement, Earl's alma mater, Lincoln University in Missouri, awarded him an honorary Doctors Degree for his many achievements in the corporate world, his contributions to his community and the honors he brought to his university. The corporations recognition of Earl's contributions? None to-date. Describing my career with IBM would not be complete if I didn't include Earl.

Defending myself against a district manager, regional manager and two division presidents made me wonder, what will be next? Even though the Division President acceded after I challenged this latest attack, past experiences indicated that they would continue with no let-up in their ferocity. I'm entering my 28th year in the business which makes me 28 years older than when I started. It's impossible for me to measure the toll the continuous battles have taken on me, both physically and mentally. Even though I feel that I can still contribute a lot to the business and to those I work with in Baltimore, I'm beginning to accept the fact that the attacks will never end while I'm in a management position.

During World War II they called it "battle fatigue". Continuous conflicts with IBM management had made me weary and I wasn't getting any younger. Was I obligated to others to continue the battle? Or was it time to pass the baton to others? The time had arrived for me to consider what would best serve my family and those who have supported me. It was also time for me to discuss and seek advise from T.G. and my good friend, Earl Wilson.

CHAPTER XIV

THE FINAL CURTAIN

The year is 1977. 1975 marked my 25th year in the business. I was then eligible to join IBM's Quarter Century Club. The usual procedure is a luncheon given by your manager, attended by eight or ten guests. You would be presented with a check, several gifts, a book filled with congratulatory letters from co-workers and executives, and a few speeches.

Since 1963, when policies changed and blacks were recruited into the business, many of them had moved into management positions. Many I had met during 100% club conventions. Many I had only spoken to by phone, especially when problems arose and they wanted to discuss them with me. I didn't always agree with them, but always made sure they understood why. If I agreed with them, from what I was told, I would encourage the caller to try once again with their manager. If that didn't work, the only avenue left was to go "open door". An executive once criticized me for what he considered "interfering". My question to him was would he prefer that they see a lawyer and go to court? The conversation was ended and the matter was never brought up again.

I mention my relationship with many black employee's throughout the country because soon after my Quarter Century Club luncheon, my friends Earl Wilson, Will Phillips, Mary Randall and others, informed me that they and other black managers were planning a week-end party to honor my 25th year in IBM. They informed me that invitations had gone out to black managers and friends throughout the country. The affair took place at a hotel in Silver Spring, Maryland and started Friday afternoon and ended Sunday Morning. They came in from everywhere, packing the hotels in Silver Spring, Maryland. Most brought their spouses. My good friend and mentor, T. G. Laster, retired and in ill health, was one of the speakers. William Clay,

Representative from Missouri and future Chairman of the House Labor committee, also spoke. I was deeply moved by the many compliments paid me, but reminded them that many in the audience were responsible for the new opportunites given to blacks when they marched, picketed, rode freedom buses and sat in at lunch counters as students. Many of those who attended were some of the "original cream of the crop" that was hired in the early 60's. Some stayed with IBM, but too many left for greater opportunities elsewhere when they realized there was a "glass ceiling" blocking their progress. ("A glass ceiling", which has now become a common phrase in the Afro-American community, is an invisible barrier many face when their in a promotable position in corporate America.)

In 1977 I was approaching my 27th year in the business and in my fifties. Concerned about the constant pressures that might be affecting my health, I was jogging 4 miles a day and working out in the local health club at least 5 days a week to escape the pressures. Baltimore was now a very strong and productive office. Losing two very experienced marketing managers hurt. The district manager's interference in the development of our newly installed marketing managers, hurt them and hurt the office. The two new marketing managers, who knew, like everyone else, that my door was always open if they had a complaint, were enticed into making criticisms that couldn't be supported.

During my meeting with the division president, I was given permission to make any changes that I felt was necessary. The new marketing managers had made unjustified complaints on their own without giving me the opportunity to explain or, if necessary, correct them. I determined that once they sensed, during the interrogation, that the district manager was searching for problems that he could use against me, they decided to play with his hand. I would have considered moving them out. Knowing the power a district manager can have over a newly installed marketing manager, I was hesitant to wreck their careers. Somehow, the word got out to other branch managers, who wondered how I could ever trust them.

Not too long after my meeting with the Division President, he called to see how things were going. I was very concerned because sometimes its difficult to keep things under cover. Word had gotten out in the district and in our office. Several managers in our office, thinking the battle was still going, came in to offer their support. This meant a lot to me, because coming out for me, they knew, could wreck their careers. My administration manager, Gary Helsel, a former marine from the Dutch countryside of Pennsylvania, said that I had always supported him and he was ready to do the same for me. Still, serving under the same bosses, who in their desire to get me out were indirectly hurting the staff in Baltimore, worried me. Failing to get a quota adjustment, despite the fact that it was proven that we were carrying part of the quota responsibility of a District of Columbia office, hurt everyone in Baltimore. Was my presence hurting a group that had always backed me 100%? These were some of the things that ran through my mind when the Division President called.

Sounding almost apologetic and assuring me that it still was my choice to make, he said that the National Alliance of Businessmen needed an executive director in Washington, D. C. and requested IBM to loan them someone to fill the position. It would be for two years and IBM would pay my salary and expenses..He also said that I could return to Baltimore as branch manager or if desired, a similar position in another location.

I said I would get back to him in a few days and made plans to discuss the situation with my good friend and mentor, T. G. Laster and Earl Wilson.

I drove to T.G.'s home in Teaneck, New Jersey. He had been retired for several years and was in ill health. Though his body was deteriorating, his mind was very sharp, as usual. Listening to T.G.,it reminded me of a statement a friend made regarding him a few years ago. "Lionel, I've been to several social gatherings where T.G. and his wife were in attendance. Every time, most of the people were gathered around T.G., listening as he gave a discourse on many subjects". Here was a mind that IBM hardly utilized but many hungered to listen to its output.

133

T.G. reminded me that for years there was only three of us, including John Lewis, and he had died before his time. He suggested that even though I may not be aware of the toll its taken on you and your family, it's like a cancer that gradually erodes your body. His message was clear. Not long after I lost a good friend and mentor.

My friend Earl Wilson never took more that 20 seconds to make his point" "Lionel, you paid your dues. Blacks are not in executive positions they should be in, but they're entrenched and have proven they can do the job. You've been in the front lines long enough. We've got some pretty sharp people in the business, so you can pass the stick to them."

After meeting with the NAB officials in Washington, I decided to accept their offer.

In the Baltimore office I felt that those I worked with were not just co-workers, but friends. To name those I considered my friends I would have to list practically the entire roster. To name those who helped and supported me, the same applies. As in Cherry Hill, the office gave me a great farewell party where my good friends had a great time "roasting" me. When being roasted, they say you laugh the hardest when the statements hit the mark. My side was aching from laughing, so I guess they constantly hit the mark. I'll never forget the toast Rex Cox made at my farewell party in Cherry Hill: "You know, when business was really bad, to keep us motivated, Lionel often referred to the novel and movie, "From the Terrace", quoting this big investment banker who, in the midst of the depression when business was almost at a standstill, looked out his window and said: "Gentlemen, as long as there's trucks running out there, there's business out there", then he would add, "fellows, the trucks are still running out there, so let's go get that business". What Lionel didn't say and didn't realize was that those trucks he saw and referred to were bringing back equipment that we sold". I almost fell off my chair laughing. The farewell party given me by the Baltimore office was also great. My Irish friend, co-worker and stellar manager, Bob Brady. with the support of others, gave me a farewell only true friends could give you. I knew I would miss the Baltimore office but at the same time hoped that the staff would benefit in the long run.

Though I was told that I could return to Baltimore, I didn't, for one minute, believe it was in the cards. Looking back, I can't imagine how I survived in corporate America this long.

EPILOGUE

I spent almost two years as executive director of the National Alliance of Business for the Greater Washington Area. There were many community projects I was involved in, the most important was a program called New Start. New Start recruited volunteers to go into the local prisons and teach those inmates who were functionally illiterate, the basics. After leaving the NAB and after retirement, I continued to do volunteer work with New Start as its president for fifteen years.

After a short loan to the Washington Urban League as a Vice President, I returned to IBM as a manager of special Markets. (As promised before I left, no offer was made to me to return to my former position or one at the same level. I later learned that the position I was given was a lower level than my previous job}

Two years after my return, IBM went through a major reorganization, merging all product divisions.

With the reorganization, the department I became part of was based in Atlanta, Ga. I remained in Bethesda, Maryland but had to commute to Atlanta frequently.

At the time of the reorganization I counted 16 black branch managers in our division. Within 3 years, only two remained as branch managers. Shortly after, of those sixteen, there were none.

In special markets, my major accomplishment was persuading IBM to acquire the "write to read" program, developed by Dr. John Henry Martin, a retired nationally known educator. This program was marketed world-wide and advertised on national T.V. The District of Columbia school system was one of the first to test the program. Their board was so impressed with the results their students achieved, they awarded me a plaque at my retirement dinner.

As a branch manager, if my office produced, it was difficult to curtail my income. Since returning to IBM and being in a salaried position, cutting me back was easy to do.

My present manager, who was based in Atlanta, kept urging me to retire. The year was 1983 and I was 61 years old and trying to maintain my healh and spirit by continuing to jogg 4 miles, 5 days a week.

I retired from IBM in January, 1984. Once again, as they did on my 25th anniversary, my friends and co-workers across the country gave me a farewell retirement party in Silver Spring, Maryland. Gordon Moodie, retired Vice President and division president, came down from New Hampshire to be one of the main speakers. Also, my good friend and representative (even though I'm not in his district) Rep. William Clay, chairman of the House Labor Committee,also was one of the main speakers.

After retiring I remained active as a volunteer with seven different organizations. I also spent two years, working part time, for the House Labor Committee. This gave me the opportunity to better understand the workings of government and the pleasure of making many new friends on the hill.

MY friend, Earl Wilson, spent five years in Paris with IBM's World Trade corporation, responsible for services to Pakistan, India, Russia, and areas of Africa. After returning to the states, Earl was placed in charge of a group marketing to distributors of IBM products. His group attained the highest quota in the country in his division and he was named division manager of the year. Despite his tremendous record of accomplishment in IBM, Earl knew that those in power would not move him up the ladder, so he took an early retirement and returned to his native city, St. Louis to fulfill his promise to return and help the underprivileged.

As the chairman and C.E.O. of Texaco stated, "Racial discrimination problems at his company represent just the tip of the iceberg". It would be a major delusion for any reader of my experiences in corporate America to think that the environment I lived in no longer exists. Today corporate America's "window dressing" is more replete. Like a tumor being treated with aspirin, present policies of many corporations in America are enjoying temporary relief from the pain while the tumor continues to grow. If Corporate America believes my experiences is something of the past and no longer exists, I suggest they ask those employee's of Texaco who filed the suit, or better, look in their our own back yard.

Unlike sixty years ago, when policies of discrimination were ignored and of little interest world-wide, today, people of every nationality and race throughout the world can focus on and create their own image of Corporate America by simply pressing the "on" button on their remote control.

IBM Poughkeepsie - Sales Class June 24, 1952

Toastmaster's International Chicago 1961

IBM Poughkeepsie 1952 - Sales Class – Graduation

Chicago South Office
Promotion Party - 1962

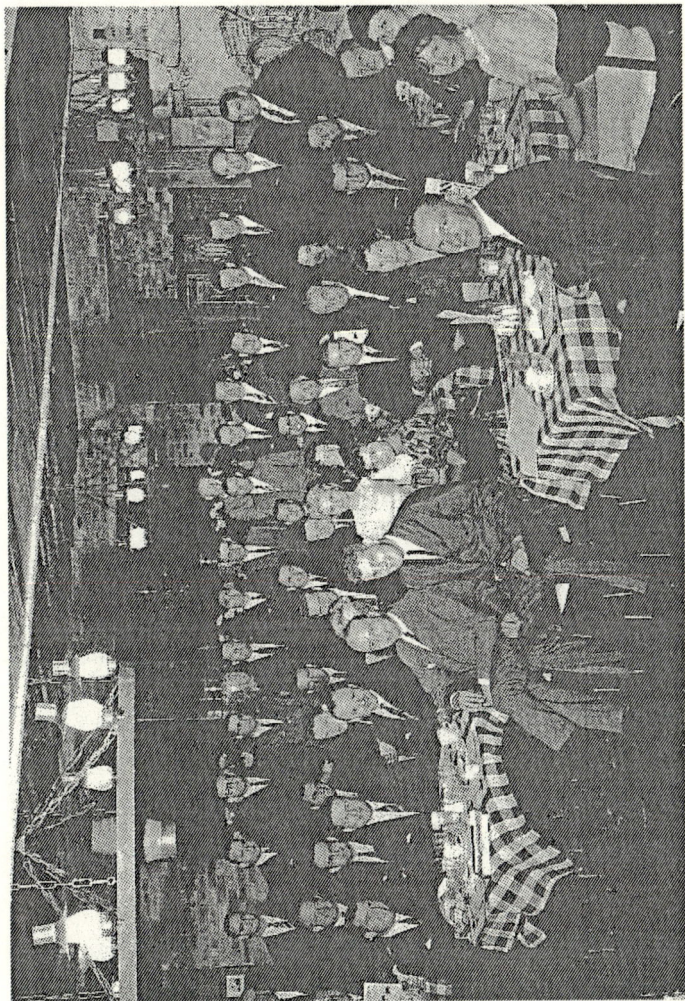

Washington Federal Office - 1963
Training Ground for Future Execs

149

1970 Cherry Hill, NJ Branch Sales Staff - Office and
Manager of the year for 2nd year in row

Earl Wilson, Will Philips, Me, T.G. (My Mentor).

Nancy and Bob Brady

1945 Liege, Belgium

Dore 6th 1944

Soldiers, Sailors and Airmen of the Allied Expeditionary Force!

You are about to embark upon the Great Crusade, toward which we have striven these many months. The eyes of the world are upon you. The hopes and prayers of liberty-loving people everywhere march with you. In company with our brave Allies and brothers-in-arms on other Fronts, you will bring about the destruction of the German war machine, the elimination of Nazi tyranny over the oppressed peoples of Europe, and security for ourselves in a free world.

Your task will not be an easy one. Your enemy is well trained, well equipped and battle-hardened. He will fight savagely.

But this is the year 1944! Much has happened since the Nazi triumphs of 1940-41. The United Nations have inflicted upon the Germans great defeats, in open battle, man-to-man. Our air offensive has seriously reduced their strength in the air and their capacity to wage war on the ground. Our Home Fronts have given us an overwhelming superiority in weapons and munitions of war, and placed at our disposal great reserves of trained fighting men. The tide has turned! The free men of the world are marching together to Victory!

I have full confidence in your courage, devotion to duty and skill in battle. We will accept nothing less than full Victory!

Good Luck! And let us all beseech the blessing of Almighty God upon this great and noble undertaking.

Dwight D Eisenhower

155

ABOUT THE AUTHOR

Born and raised in Newark, New Jersey. The youngest of four children of James and Alice Fultz. Entered army in August of 1943 and transferred to England in December, 1943. After serving in five campaigns with the 3rd Army, returned to the states and discharged in January, 1946. Joined IBM in 1950 and entered sales in 1951. Received many awards, including IBM's Outstanding Achievement Award and Manager of the Year three times. Did volunteer work with many community organizations, among them NEW START. New Start was a volunteer organization centered in the District of Columbia metropolitan area, that worked to rehabilitate prison inmates through education. He served as its President for fifteen years. Early in his retirement, he also worked for two years assisting the Chairman of the House Labor Committee, Rep. William Clay of Missouri. Mr. Fultz is married, with two daughters and one stepson.